The Broadbot Letters

The Broadbottom Letters

Richard !

You have displayed great
wisdom in purchasing
this magnificent book.
Long life and success to
you Sir

Alun 'Broadbottom' Ward.

By

Alun Broadbottom Ward

First published in 2013 by
Broadbottom Ward Publishing

ISBN 978-0-9574343-0-1

If you would like a copy of this book direct from the author,
please email me at buythisbooknow@aol.com

Typeset and produced by
The Studio Publishing Services Ltd
www.publishingservicesuk.co.uk

Printed and bound by CPI Group (UK) Ltd, Croydon, CR0 4YY

About the Author

Alun Broadbottom Ward was born of humble stock. Educated insufficiently, he entered into, and exited from, a series of disastrous commercial ventures during his formative years.

Currently the chief scientist at Britain's only Concrete Teeth Design Establishment, he is also President of the Devon Parsnip Alliance.

Thrice married, thrice divorced, Ward expounds unwanted theories and opinions on a variety of matters, to all manner of people, companies and institutions. A pest indeed to the recipients of the Letters in this book.

Broadbottom Ward lives quietly in the south west of England with partner Grizzelda, along with 27 chickens and 4 ducks, all also called Grizzelda.

I do hope this book sells millions as I am on a final written warning from my employer.

My manager, (Mr Glue), yes . . . that is his real name, will then be told where to "stick" his job.

Until then he is a fine and honourable man. His word is his "bond". An inspirational and progressive leader of the highest calibre, "adhering" to his principles at all times.

Reviews

"Very Funny" . . . *Group Captain MD Chomper*

"The People in this book are unbelievable" . . . *Gary Goon*

Posing as a retired Wing Commander, Emeritus Professor or addled old Lady, the Author has pestered dozens of innocent Companies and Associations for opinion and advice.

The ultimate anti theft device for a car, the answers to those questions that Bakers never dare ask, the winner of "Mr Sausages 1956" and the advice given to a newly elected Member of Parliament are within the pages of this year's funniest book.

"The Author is off his head" . . . *Florissa Harmiston Pond.*

"He wrote to me, the swine, and was very rude and insulting" . . . *A. Cod.*

"He is one of our funniest minds" . . . *Trevor Crunch, Head Scientist at The Institute for Cracker Research.*

Dedication

This book is dedicated to my two daughters, Wendy and Victoria

Also to my grandchildren, Billy, Paige, Shannon, Henry, Davy and Kirsty

A special thank you to Paige who helped with ideas

A very special thank you to Michael Pommeroy Huggins who's
constant interference was invaluable

Most of all. A big thank you to all those who
replied to my letters, some who outdid the senders enquiry,
with pithy and humorous replies

The Manager .
The Riviera Hotel ,
Bridge Road ,
MAIDENHEAD .
SL6 8DW .

Group Captain MD Chomper (ret).
Copperwalls Lodge ,
DEVON
27 - 01 - 2010 .

Sir ,

Many years ago , late july1954 to be precise , I had the great pleasure of dining at , and indeed staying the night , at your excellent hotel .
The occasion was a squadron do , one or two of the chaps leaving the service , that sort of thing . Good dinner , Port , you know the form .
The Manager , (or his Adjutant) , was a fellow called Martin , Lartin , or Fargo as I recall . Fine chap , joined in , made the night go with a swing .
We did arrange for another rank to attend the night as photographer , and he took dozens of snaps of the assemblage . Martin also took quite a few pictures , for what he called promotional purposes , to be retained at the Hotel .
From memory , I think the photos from our man were distributed between our chaps , and we selected 5 or so each .
Self , snotty Parker , and Ginger Granger were the chaps at the hub of things , and I think Parker paid the bill .
Trouble is , old chap , one is now in ones nineties and have jolly well lost the bally snaps I had .
In true RAF tradition , Ginger has bought it , and Snotty wiped his last twenty odd years ago . So replacements , from ones former chums , out of the question .
Wondering therefore , if Lartin did pack the old pics in the hotel vault , or have they gone for the proverbial ?.
Would be prepared to pay a few bob for any photos , if you have any , although after this long I hold out little hope .

Date . Around 20 - 31st July 1954 . Thursday night as I recall .

Guests .   Grp Cap MD Chomper . Wing Co Charles (snotty) Parker .
            Grp Cap Greville (ginger) Granger . Miss Hilda Potter .
            Miss Barnes . and Mr Julian Fontaine .
I do hope you can come up with some sort of result .
In your hands as it were , appreciate efforts , would make an old man very happy . Good fortune to you sir . Carry on the good work .

I remain , Group Captain Michael David Chomper , at your service .

RIVIERA HOTEL

Group Captain MD Chomper (ret.)
Copperwalls Lodge,

Devon

Paul Bryan
The Thames Riviera Hotel
Bridge Road
Maidenhead
SL6 8DW

06th February 2010

Dear Group Captain Michael David Chomper (ret.)

Thank you for your letter dated, 27th January 2010. I have had a look in our archive store for you, but, unfortunately, our records and storage does not go back that far. And, as we have changed ownership a few times since your visit, I'm afraid; your pictures may have been lost in the ownership change over's we have gone through.

Once again, I apologise, for not being able to help you, and wish you luck in finding your lost pictures.

If, I can be of any future use, please feel free to contact me anytime.

Yours truly,

Paul Bryan
Duty Manager
The Thames Riviera Hotel
Bridge Road
Maidenhead
SL6 8DW

Tel: (01628) 674 057

"bespoke"

The Thames Riviera Hotel · Bridge Road · Maidenhead · Berkshire SL6 8DW
T: 01628 674 057 · **F:** 01628 776 586
E: res.thamesriviera@bespokehotels.com · **www.**bespokehotels.com/thamesriviera
Galleon Taverns Limited Company Registered in England & Wales at 25 Harley Street, London W1G 9DR Registration No. 01191 280
belong. beloved. bespoke.

DEBRETT'S
18-20 HILL RISE ,
RICHMOND ,
SURREY TW10 6UA .

Donald Rawbone .
Copperwalls Lodge
DEVON .
28 - 12 - 2008 .

RE - ETIQUETTE .

Dear Sir /Modom ,

Would you be so good as to inform one , (me) , how
to say , naff off in a posh manner .
I understand Her Highness The Princess Royal once used the words to
great effect .
I need this information in order to deliver the phrase in person to
somebody who richly deserves it .
Would it be , Naff Owf , ?   Should I accompany the rebuke with a tirade
of swearing and obsenities ?. Or should one remain composed and calm
Being a working class lad , I have had no posh education like , I very
much need your advice .
One looks forward to ones reply .

I Have the privilege to be sir , and shall remain , your obedient servant.

Donald Rawbone .   *Mr Rawbone*

- 4 -

Mr Donald Rawbone
Copperwalls Lodge

Devon

7 . 1 . 2009

Dear Mr Rawbone

Thank you for your letter of 28th December.

Concerning your question about the rebuke of your acquaintance, we are all in agreement that you should emulate HRH The Princess Royal, whose pithy 'naff off' to assembled scabby journalists caused a sensation in the British press some years ago.

Our only slight concern is your suggested pronunciation, 'Naff Owf', which (a) could betray your working class roots, or (b) be interpreted by your enemy as a phrase in some foreign language.

The accepted upper class pronunciation and spelling is of course 'Naff Orf', and this should be used whenever necessary. We suggest that this rebuke should only be followed by a stream of invective if, like HRH, you are on horseback and can immediately dash off into the Devonshire countryside.

Yours sincerely

CHARLES KIDD

Ed Peerage & Baronetage

Debrett's Limited
18-20 Hill Rise
Richmond
Surrey TW10 6UA
United Kingdom

Telephone +44 (0)20 8939 2050
Fax +44 (0)20 8939 2051
people@debretts.co.uk
www.debretts.co.uk

The New Talent Section .
Mahoney Bannon Associates ,
Concorde House ,
18 Margaret Street ,
Brighton & Hove .
BN2 1TS .

Funny Willie Wilkinson .
Copperwalls Lodge ,
DEVON .

13 - 04 - 2010 .

Dear Sir ,
      I am a comedian and impressionist . My impression of Terry Thomas , (the cad) , is said by many to be hilarious . I also do Charlie Chester , Arthur Haynes , and an excellent Clement Attlee .
My Margaret Lockwood is peerless , I can also do Pol Pot and all of the Little Rascals . My Harold Wilson has been likened to that of Mike Yarwood . This has been mentioned many times .
I do the "next door neighbour" joke very well , although I don't really understand it . You know the one , where he exhibits his parrots and canaries at local shows , but is most enthusiastic about showing off his twelve finches .
I also sing and dance to a modest degree , my speciality being hitting the high notes in "sugar baby love" , the chart topper by the Rubettes in 1974 .
I have long curly green hair , have a range of humorous hats and props , along with a hideous laugh . My knees are incredibly knobbly ,
I have a gap between my first pre molar and second incisor , in which , I can balance cutlery , spanners and even a cricket bat .
I have stopped juggling sharp knives on the advice of my doctor , but would happily chance it again if it would give my career a kick start .
My current partner , Yao , has suggested that I try to perfect the "catching the bullet in the teeth trick" , but I cannot figure out just how to practice this in any sort of safety , Yao has agreed to fire the gun though , so I am partly there on that score .
One or two of my friends have said that I will never make it .
I think they are wrong , please give me your opinion , as professionals in the entertainment industry .
Could I make it ? .
I do have a day job , but currently have no agent , could you represent me and find engagements for me .

Please reply soon ,   yours most sincerely , Funny Willie Wilkinson .

Willie .

Concorde House
18 Margaret Street
Brighton BN2 1TS

Tel: 01273 685970 / 672262
Fax: 01273 685971 / 818306

info@mbagency.co.uk
mbagency.co.uk

14th April 2010

Mr. Funny Willie Wilkinson,
Copperwalls Lodge,
Whitestone,
DEVON EX4 2HT

Dear Mr Wilkinson,

Thank you for your most interesting letter.

There is a definite shortage of the calibre of comedian that you portray. This seems to equal the shortage of venues willing to take a chance with good old-fashioned Music Hall and Variety.

I well remember the days of Monday Night Music Hall at Lambeth Town Hall with the wonderful Dennis Ploughwright as the MD. Every evening at band call he would summon me over to the pit and ask me how to keep a poofter in suspense; when I informed him that I didn't know, he would say "I'll tell you next week love!" I never quite understood the context of this weekly ritual but I assumed it was a music hall tradition.

One week I booked 'Dash's TV Chimps' from that nice Jean Salburg, whose father Leon was the resident ghost at the Alex theatre in Birmingham. We only managed one performance because the big 5' chimp, who was the star of the "Piano's on my foot" / "Cooooeee Mister Shifter" Tetley Tea advert took an instant dislike to Johnny Fuller, our drummer. He would lean over into the pit open his mouth and show all his teeth then spin round quickly and blow raspberries with the other end (the chimp, not Johnny). They were great nights and by the end of the show, Dennis would accompany with his feet on either end of the piano to avoid the river of urine running down the stalls into the pit from our older patrons and the few regulars from the Trinity Arms round the corner, so, we had no musical expression for the finale!

You have obviously worked hard on your act and I know the pain you may have gone through. I am excited by the gap in your teeth and wondered if you could manage impressions of George Formby (in profile of course). I would suggest 'Fanlight Fanny', but that would have to be your choice, of course.

I can tell you that the bullet in the teeth trick is a little hard to manage and comes with a bit of a health warning. There is a foreboding tale of the act going disastrously wrong at the Empire, Brighton, many years ago when the man was shot and the bullet ricocheted off the gold tooth of Woo Flung Dung the Chinese magician (actually Herbert Tawt from Oswaldtwistle) with a stick on Chinese moustache and a very ornate oriental dressing gown he bought from Oscar Wilde because Oscar had no need for it in Reading. There was a drum roll and a gasp from the audience when the shot was fired, the ricochet bullet hit the gold tooth pinged off and shot round the auditorium knocking the nipples off of those rude plaster ladies holding up the boxes, parting the hair of a large gin-soaked man in the circle, who had only come to see this act and ended up entering the forehead of a young lad on the front of the gallery, who had just stood up to relieve himself on the richer folk below. However, the critic was so drunk he started an avalanche of applause that is still talked about today! If I were you I would get your partner Yao to take out a very large insurance on your life and the lives of the audience before you perform.

I would love to see you 'do' Arthur Haynes: I have fond memories of Arthur because he was on the bill the night my Father let the Theatre Royal Rochdale burn down. It ended the weeks run on a Wednesday and Tessie

Derek (Bo) Keller, Andrea Todd, Stephen Holroyd, Alan Kite
Formerly John Mahoney Management

O'Shea lost her ukulele that week. I always thought my Dad was speaking in euphemism until I saw her at Blackpool Opera House with only her banjo.

I think the Clem Attlee act may be a little like a Tory government in today's political market, past its time, and ‌ of bovine waste. Have you thought about an impersonation of the Thatcher woman, in the vein of Old Mother Riley, ending up with a full mad scene and a full frontal lobotomy then the apotheosis of the act, sending a tas‌ force to an island nobody has heard of to get good results in the next election, or do you think that is a bit real Anyway I am sure with your talent you will be able to knock 'em in the aisles or shoot them depending on your act.

My only reserve, and it is only a slight one, is the colour of your hair. I wondered if you had ever thought of having all your hair shaved off with a lipstick dot in the centre and going on stage as (just for a bit of a gag yo‌ understand) a right tit. I think that would get a laugh.

Please let me know where you are working next so I can come to your gig and take the piss out of you at wor‌

Your very own

Stephen Holroyd.

Head of New and Exciting Talent.

PS. Thank you so much for not sticking the stamp on your letter too well, It was not franked and we managed‌ prise the stamp off for this reply. Our boss is the meanest man in the world when it comes to stamps, he wou‌ go crackers if he knew we used a 1st class stamp on this letter. "2nd ull do" he would say. It comes from his upbringing in Yorkshire where they were so poor they had no money for medicines or food, If he was were constipated, the old man from next door used to sit him on a potty and tell him ghost stories and the walls we‌ so thin, if you poked the fire, you could have a bloke off his bicycle in the street and he told me that his moth‌ opened the oven door one Sunday and the bloke form next door was dipping his bread in their gravy. It was ‌ little village called Garfroth, so rough, that Kate Adie was the barmaid and the only roast they served on a Sunday was broken led of lamb!

It's a much better place now but the M62 is still cobbled round there.

So thanks,

The Managing Director .
Ropes and Twines ,
TIMCO Ltd ,
Unit 3 Organsdale Farm ,
Tarporley ,
Kelsall ,
CHESHIRE CW6 0SR .

Wing commander Jacob Fall (ret) .
Copperwalls Lodge ,
DEVON
24 - 03 - 2010 .

Dear Ropes and Twines ,

I am an adventurer of old . A fearless , and foolish Climber , Diver , flier , and retired servant of Her Majesty .
You may recall my adventures in the South Seas in the 1950s , when I was oft seen appearing from the deep with a handful of Doubloons , or part of a rusted cannon . The natives referred to me as the as "the White Shark".
My ship , The Boris , was designed , built and Skippered by me .
Maybe you remember my exploits of the 1960s , when I was the first to Wingwalk naked , atop a 1922 Vickers bi - plane , piloted by a triple amputee , flown by him whilst drunk , into the teeth of a force nine blizzard against air traffic control advice .
For the last few years now I have been scaling the west wing of the Lodge here , with , and without ropes . Gaining experience , and gathering confidence as I progress , to the point where I am now planning my next conquest . A foolish quest maybe , but I have the support of the remaining members of the "Retired adventurers club" , who convene monthly at the local pub , "The Duck and Parsnip" in the village every third Wednesday of the month .
Huggins , the Cobbler , has undertaken to provide boots .
The local country store owner , has promised Arctic clothing , and provisions . The local vet , (a Bronze medalist from the 1956 Olympics), will provide Dogs . But as yet , we have no rope Sponsor , and need one .
Your excellent Company , with its renown for top quality equipment was the first to come to mind .
By providing rope for the expedition , your company would have prominent logo space at the top , and indeed bottom , of , wait for it ….
EVEREST . Yes , we intend to scale Everest , from its North West route .
The possibilities to promote your Company in this venture are , as I am sure you will agree , endless .
"Ropes and Twines make Everest ascent possible" , that sort of thing , your advertising boys will have a field day , the chance of a lifetime .
Well sir , we need 29,029 feet of rope , are you in ? .

Yours , in anticipation of your participation , Wingco Fall .

THERE WAS NO REPLY TO THIS LETTER . The Wing Commander
had no need for rope after all , He fell from the East wing of the Lodge the
very next day .
(Wing Commander Fall)

The Egyptology department ,
THE BRITISH MUSEUM ,
Great Russell Street ,
LONDON WC1B 3DG .
25-11-2008

Dr Wolfgang Flaerts .
Copperwalls lodge ,

DEVON

Dear Sir ,

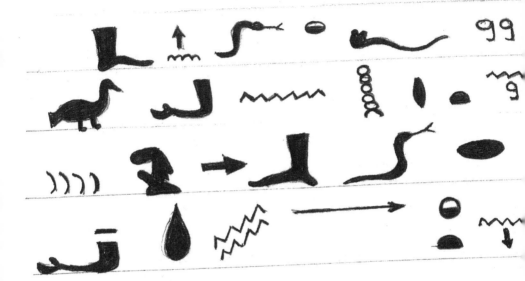

Yours Sincerely Wolfgang Flaerts.

THE
BRITISH
MUSEUM

Dr. Wolfgang Flaerts
Copperwalls Lodge

Devon

11 December 2008

Dear Sir,

⌣‿⌣

Yours sincerely,

Marcel Marée
Assistant Keeper

Employment Tribunal Advice .
Dalton House ,
60 Windsor Avenue ,
LONDON .
SW19 2RR .

Mr Richard Fiddler .
Copperwalls Lodge ,

DEVON .

14 - 04 - 2010 .

Dear Sir / Madam ,

        I hope that your company can give me some advice on the problem I have with my employer .

I work as a Plumber with a local maintenance company . Recently a new Contracts Manager has been appointed , he likes to think he is the " new broom " , that will sweep the firm clean .

He has , to say the least , an aggressive style of management .

He has introduced a " useless Bastard of the week " chart , aimed at motivating employees to improve , " efficiency " .

This chart is pinned to the office wall when we arrive in the morning , but is removed after we go off to work on site , this is to avoid him being criticised for it by his superiors .

He refers to two of our Plumbers as "pair of knuckle dragging hairy arsed shithouse mechanics" .

Refers to our two joiners as Gripper and Butt head .

Uses phases such as , " if they work , I pay them , if they don't the buggers are out that door pronto " .

He has frequent outburst of violent and aggressive behaviour .

Has struck one of the Painters , and has kicked the apprentice Joiner up the arse one more than one occasion , (he is only 17) .

He says he is fireproof and untouchable , he rules by fear , he also alters to stock sheets in order to steal materials . On three separate days , men have been challenged to fight him , " in the car park " , two accepted and have received severe beatings .

Since his appointment , 12 men lave left or been sacked , out of an initial workforce of 26 .

This man is a recently demobbed Royal Marine Commando , and freely admits to have killed . He has a glint in his eye when mentioning this .

He has abolished the bonus system , and has made it clear we DO NOT stop for lunch , and that , "any of you soft bastards that do are out with my toe up your jacksie" .

All complaints to Head Office seem to go unheeded .

I have enclosed a £5 note to cover at least , your reply , as I assume you could not help .

Please advise if you can , with regards , Richard Fiddler

tribunalonline
protecting your employment rights

Dalton House
60 Windsor Avenue
London
SW19 2RR

Telephone: 0800 840 54 40
Facsimile: 01656 673 361
www.tribunal-online.com
enquiries@tribunal-online.com

Tribunal Online is a trading title of
Adroit Direct (UK) Limited
Registered Address: Fields House
Square Park, Ferginett, Bridgend, CF35 5LJ
Company Registration Number 06784539
Registered VAT Number 941 858 435
Regulated by the Ministry of Justice

A Member of Fields Group

Richard Fiddler
Copperwalls Lodge

Devon

23rd April 2010

Dear Richard Fiddler,

Thank you for your letter dated the 14th of April 2010. Unfortunately, we are unable to help you with your request in the format provided, however please contact us on 0800 8405440 in order to purchase our services.

Please find enclosed your letter and payment of £5.00.

Kind regards,

Tribunal Online

- 13 -

The Advice Department .
The National Soil Resources Centre ,
Building 53 ,
Cranfield University ,
CRANFIELD ,
BEDFORDSHIRE MK43 0AL .

Derek Mudd .
Copperwalls Lodge ,
DEVON .
30 - 05 - 2010 .

Dear Mr Head of the Advice department , or Ms Head of the Advice department ,

My name is Derek Mudd , and I am , 9 , years old .
In about three or 4 weeks we are going to do farming and food growing studies at school . Miss Tucker , our teacher , has said that I am not trying hard enough some times , but I am . MY Dad says that she fails to see true potential in the lad . My Mother said that she wears her clothes too tight , and that will impair Her judgement .

So I decided to speak to my Granddad about it . He says that if I get a head start on the other oiks , I will impress the mistress , and it always worked when he was a young Rake .
So , can you tell me what SOIL IS ? HOW DID IT get there ? What is it made of ? Granddad says that it is really old food and leaves , and a bit of droppings , (he said another word that will offend people) , so I wont say it .
Granddad was in WARS , and says he has been horribly scarred , although I have only seen one small scar on his elbow .

Can you also , let me know just one key bit of information that will impress Miss Tucker , and show her I am not a thicky .
Granddad says that I should " go to the very top if you want info boy " .
That is why I am writing to you , you are the TOP , of soil and growing matters .
Granddad has great wisdom . He is always telling me that . He has massive experience and studied at the University of Life .
I think that is in Yorkshire , because he was born there , I think he is over 70 , and has been to a lot of different countries when he was younger . My mother knows he is incontinent .
Granddad grows Beans , Cabbages , Leeks and onions , so he knows a bit about soil .
Please write back soon .

Yours sir , or Madam , most sincerely . Derek .

DEREK

Master Derek Mudd
Copperwalls Lodge

Devon

Dear Derek,

RE: SOIL

How nice to hear from you and of your interest in SOIL, farming and food growing. It must be something to do with your family name and inheritance. We here at NSRI are sure that, although the answer undoubtedly always lies in the SOIL, your jeans also have a lot to do with it. It is important not to get ones that are too tight (ask your Granddad about that, he sounds like a very wise man). Like your mum, we suspect that this is the problem with your teacher, Miss Tucker, although we should quite like to meet her just to check this out.

We think you must be a really clever young lad (not an oik at all) to ask advice from your Granddad as it is a well known fact that all SOIL knowledge lies with elderly and rather smelly old men known as 'Greybeards'. It is a pity about your Granddad's incontinence. Although he clearly knows a bit about soil, his knowledge of the digestive tract seems less good. Maybe you should suggest that he eats less of the beans, cabbages, leeks and onions that he grows in his garden? We also suggest that he consumes less of the wonderful 'coider' that is made in your part of the country.

Anyway, you have certainly come to the right place to get an answer to your questions. As you say, we are definitely TOPP of soil and growing matters. The first questions you ask are therefore an absolute doddle for us: 'What is SOIL and how did it get there?'

As everyone nose GOD made the world in six days and on the seventh she rested (weekends were shorter then). However, whilst she was taking her ease down at the Pub at the end of the Universe, she suddenly realized that she had forgotten to take the EARTH out of the cosmic oven in which she had placed it to brown off ready for human habitation. Dashing back home (heaven/hell as it is known) she whipped it out of the cosmic oven only to discover that the outside was now too hard and almost black! In an effort to soften it up, she poured oil all over it. Unfortunately, most of this oil sank inside and stayed there (until BP managed to drill down and find it again), so she rubbed in some soot, face plumping cream and a bit of navel fluff and this seemed to do the trick. Just to make sure that the softening process had worked, she added 10 trillion microbes known as 'grey goo' to work their magic. The resulting surface now looked ideal for human beans to live off and she decided to call it SOIL, a mixture of 'soot' and 'oil'. She couldn't be arsed to work in the names of all the other stuff she had used as, by then, she really needed another beer at the Pub at the end of the Universe.

We hope this answers your first questions.

As to giving you a key piece of information about SOIL to impress your teacher, if the answer above does not do this, then we suggest you try the following:

If you dig down into the soil to about 1m depth and clean off one of the sides of the hole, you will see a series of roughly horizontal layers of different colour. This is known as a SOIL Profile and it is possible to extract a slice of this profile and preserve it on a tray. Technically this slice is called a MONOLITH. Here at the Advice Department, we are very proud of our 'Monoliths' and, if your teacher is sufficiently impressed by this key fact, she may want to come up and see us sometime and we will show her some particularly fine examples.

So there you are, the collected wisdom of the Advice Department of the TOPP department of soil and growing matters has come up trumps (ask Granddad about this technical term) again. If this doesn't put you in Miss Tucker's good books we don't know what will (be advised, the apple does not work).

Please don't feel that you have to send us wads of cash for this advice but, just in case you feel happy with our response, our fees are £2,000-00 per minute. We are sure that Mr. Michael Gove at the Dept. of Education will be only too happy to pay.

With very best regards,

Mr. or Ms. *Peat*

Head of Advice Department

PS — we liked your vegetable patch. The bee
are coming along just fine!

Norma Dobney .
National Association of Flower Arrangers ,
Osborne House ,
12 Devonshire Square ,
LONDON EC2M 4TE .

Wilfred Hornpipe (chairman)
The WDCWYT Club ,
Copperwalls Lodge ,
DEVON
14 - 06 - 2010 .

My Dear Norma ,

May I say what a beautiful name that is , and I am sure
you are a most delightful lady , with charm and grace .
However , I must inform you that we , at the WDCWYT Club , have no
interest in floral arrangements whatever . We care not for them .
Our Club , " We Don't Care What You Think Club " , care not in the least
about your club , and or , Association . Frankly , it stinks .
As Chairman , I can assure you , that your organisation will NOT be
receiving one of our professionally printed Christmas cards .
WHY ? You may ask . Well , it is for the simple reason that I , nor any of
my members , (some of which are rich and powerful) , give not a fig for
your rabble of Floralists . BAH !
Our Club , objects to all clubs and affiliations of all types , at all times .
As a boy I was forced to tend Dahlia's , a passion of my late father , as
was growing onions . Damn those onions .
I have written to the Onion association , and given them hell ,
we criticised their beloved product mercilessly , be under no illusion .
May I add at this juncture that , I find that Norma is the most enchanting
name , and should any of my Daughters bless the family with another
granddaughter in future , I do hope that the child may be called Norma .
Delightful , absolutely delightful .
Back to the point , Damn your Flowers , and damn your bally floral
arrangement Association . I am against it , do you hear me ? , against it !
You and your fellow flora - o'philes aught to get proper jobs , and stop
silly old fools like me , having to waste the abundant time that I have In
retirement from complaining about you .
I have enclosed a first class stamp to enable you to reply to this letter .
Our club funds are vast and can afford such gestures .
All of our current membership are retired military types , old Etonians ,
business men , and a frightening assortment of old farts .
Prospective new members are never encouraged to apply .
Annual subscription to our club is astronomical , so don't ask to join .
I wish only to shield you from the inevitable black ball .
I have enjoyed the privilege to write to my dear Norma .
I remain your obedient servant ,
Wilfred Hornpipe.

THERE WAS NO REPLY TO THIS LETTER . Hornpipe cares not
about this , and continues to annoy people to this day .
(Wilfred Hornpipe)

The Concrete Society .
Riverside House ,
4 Meadows Business Park ,
Station Approach ,
Blackwater ,
CAMBERLEY ,
SURREY GU17 9AB .

Alfred Blocker .
Copperwalls Lodge ,
DEVON .
28 - 11 - 2010 .

Dear Sir ,

I would very much appreciate some advice regarding the strength of concrete . The mix ratio , and the setting time for a project I am currently undertaking .

I am over 70 years old and have had false teeth for some 45 years .

During that time I have lost or broken some 12 sets of dentures . This has cost me a fortune over the years .

Using an old plate from a broken pair of dentures , I propose to mould into them , a strong concrete mix , to make a powerful set of teeth .

I have assumed that using any aggregate in the mix is impossible , as the large pebbles would prevent a smooth finish on such small units of concrete .

Sharp sand and cement is my favoured recipe , some 4 sharp sand to one cement .   What do you think ?.

I propose to compress the concrete into the moulds by means of a small dental drill to expel the air from the mix prior to setting .

When set , I could polish the edge on a smooth grind wheel , incorporating a sharp edge for grinding tougher foods .

Could you please also advise me on any additive I could safely use to make the teeth whiter than just the usual grey concrete colour .

The chaps down at the day centre think it's a fantastic idea , and a few are envious . Some are sceptical , and one thinks I am completely barmy.

I t has now become something of a challenge , and indeed an obsession .

I do hope that you don't think I am a old fool , with a daft , impossible idea .

I would appreciate any advice you may have for me .

Yours sincerely   Alf Blocker .

The Concrete Society
Riverside House
4 Meadows Business Park
Station Approach
Blackwater, Camberley
Surrey GU17 9AB

Mr A Blocker
Copperwalls Lodge
...
Devon

Tel: +44 (0) 1276 607140
Fax: +44 (0) 1276 607141
DDI: **+44 (0)1276 607140**

9 December 2008   Rid/Blocker-1

Dear Mr Blocker

Thank you for your letter dated 29 November 2008 concerning concrete dentures.

As a material for construction, concrete in all its forms is a strong and durable material. Its strength lies in the fact that it has good compressive strength, but its weakness is in its tensile strength. Tensile strength is very important as it provides resistance to bending and shearing forces. In this respect concrete is cast with steel reinforcement in the tensile zone.

I fear that dentures will have little tensile strength if made with concrete. A sand cement mortar as you suggest will not with stand the rigors of chewing. Even if special cements and admixtures are used to improve the compressive strength, and hence tensile strength which is roughly 10% of the compressive, we have doubts that you will be successful.

However, don't let this put you off – it will be an interesting project even if the result becomes a life size sculpture.

Yours sincerely

Richard Day
On behalf of Concrete Society

enquiries@concrete.org.uk
http://www.concrete.org.uk

Limited by Guarantee
Registered in London: 884419
Registered Office: as above

The Concrete Advisory Service (CAS) is a trading brand wholly owned subsidiary of The Concrete Society Limited

Birdlife advice .
Seaview Wildlife Encounter ,
Oakhill Road ,
Springvale ,
SEAVIEW ,
Isle Of Wight PO34 5AP ..

Mrs Florissa Harmiston - Pond .
Copperwalls Lodge ,
DEVON .
14 - 06 - 2010 .

Dear Birdlife Advisor ,

I am so pleased I was able to find your address , as I need some advice regarding a Pelican , I do so hope you can help . For some 3 weeks we here at the Lodge , have had a daily visit from a large Pelican , and initially the bird was a joy to see .
The Pelican has now decided to " move in " with our resident flock of chickens . We also keep Ducks .
The bird , (very large) , eats more corn than our 15 Chickens would collectively consume on a daily basis .
Although the Pelican is a joy to see , he , (or she) , is a voracious eater . The Bird is presumably , off course , as we are some 5 miles from the nearest coastline . Some 5 miles nor-nor east from Topsham Bay .
Having lost one's Husband some years ago , the task of identification of these visiting birds falls to me , and I am less proficient than my late husband Hubert .
Hubert was most accomplished in bird identification .
Entering my 99th year , one has enough difficulty identifying one's own dogs sometimes , I have four . Never mind those bally birds .

Huggins the Gardener , himself aged , has given his opinion that our bird maybe a Heron of some sort .
I have told him he is an old fool . So far no Chickens have been taken , and our Duck population remains stable , although we have lost a Quail .

Could your good company give advice to relocate our wayward Pelican ?

I do hope you can help with some good advice

Florissa Harmiston - Pond .

Seaview Wildlife Encounter
Oakhill Road
Seaview
Isle of Wight
PO34 5AP

Mrs Florissa Harmiston-Pond

Copperwalls Lodge

DEVON

16 June 2010

Dear Mrs Harmiston-Pond

Thank you for your recent letter regarding the suspected arrival of a Pelican on your property near Topsham Bay.

Would it be possible for you to forward a photograph of this bird to assist us in confirming its identification and then recommending a possible course of action? If you have access to a digital camera an image could be attached to an email (our email address is: info@seaviewwildlife.com or if not then posted as you did with your letter.

This is a most unusual story and one that we would be pleased to assist you with if at all possible.

If you are contactable by phone or email I would be most grateful if you would contact us with this information.

I shall be away from the Park for the next few days, returning Monday 28th June. In my absence please would you liaise with Lorraine Adams, one of the Park's Directors. Lorraine's mobile number is: 07811 560790.

Looking forward to hearing from you.

Yours sincerely

Jules Brittan

General Manager

Lorraine Adams .
Seaview Wildlife Encounter ,
Oakhill Road ,
Springvale ,
SEAVIEW ,
Isle Of Wight PO34 5AP ..

Mrs Florissa Harmiston - Pond .
Copperwalls Pelicanlodge ,
DEVON .
19 - 06 - 2010 .

Dear Lorraine ,
      Your colleague Jules Brittan , was good enough to reply very promptly , to my enquiry regarding a Pelican visiting my garden . The Pelican has flown , and indeed walked , into my garden quite a few times since my writing to you on Monday last .

My Great Granddaughter Clarissa , has managed to reproduce the photographs I have , onto paper .
I have enclosed two of them for you to study .
My nearest neighbour Mr Barking , a Smallholder who lives about a mile and a half away , opined that it was an Albatross or a Coot of some sort . Mr Barking however , has a serious visual impairment , and his testimony cannot be relied upon . He is also over 90 and somewhat unreliable in all his functions .
I eagerly await your expert opinion on what we can do with this Pelican .

Yours Sincerely Florissa Hermiston - Pond .

F H Pond

- 22 -

SEAVIEW WILDLIFE ENCOUNTER   Flamingo Park (Seaview) Ltd.

Reg Office: Lamorna,
Oakhill Road, Springvale,
Seaview, Isle Of Wight.
PO34 5AP
VAT NO: 938 3236 09
Tel: 01983 612153
Fax: 01983 613465
Email: info@seaviewwildlife.com
Reg No: 6632691

Mrs. Florrisa Harmiston-Pond,   24th June, 2010
Copperwalls Lodge,

DEVON.

Dear Mrs. Harmiston-Pond,

Thank you for your letter received with the images of the mystery bird.

Sadly, it is not a pelican but an Indian Peafowl (a peacock!) These are quite common now and many people keep them as pets in small holdings and gardens. We have quite a few at the Park and they are quite spectacular when showing off to their mates with their beautiful tail feathers opened out.

I have enclosed a couple of postcards from our Park - one with an image of our pelican and one with the image of a peacock with the beautiful fan of tail feathers.

The best advice I can offer is that if the bird is being a nuisance then contacting your local RSPCA officer and asking their advice on moving the bird or finding the owner would be the best course of action.

If you continue to feed the peacock it will most definitely keep returning to your garden as it is getting very well fed and well looked after!

I do hope that this has been of some help to you,

Kind regards,

L. Adams/

Miss Lorraine Adams (Director)
Seaview Wildlife Encounter

PeLICAN
Bottom right
image

Nigh

PUBLISHED BY: W. J. NIGH & SONS LTD.
SANDOWN I.W. COPYRIGHT
Website: www.nigh.co.uk

5 032510 800011

FLAMINGO PARK
WILDLIFE ENCOUNTER
SEAVIEW, ISLE OF WIGHT
Phone (01983) 612153
Top left: Snowy Owl. Top right: Red Squirrel.
Lower left: Rainbow Lorikeets feeding nectar,
courtesy Cage & Aviary Birds. Lower centre:
Beaver. Lower right: Pink-Backed Pelican.
WJN 1957

Peacock
Bottom left
image

FLAMINGO PARK
WILDLIFE ENCOUNTER
SEAVIEW, ISLE OF WIGHT
Phone (01983) 612153
Top left: Mute Swan with Cygnet – photo Mr.
Nigel, Kendal-Ward. Top centre: Hawaiian
Geese. Top right: Barnacle Geese with Goslings.
Bottom left: Displaying Peacock. Bottom right:
Domestic Geese – photo S. J. Trott.
WJN 1956

Nigh

Mr Andrew Fletcher .
Anixter Components ,
Nimrod Way ,
West Dorst Parade Park ,
Wimborne ,
DORSET BH21 7HY .

The Mighty Horrendo .
Copperwalls Lodge ,
DEVON .
22 - 08 - 2011

Dear Mr Fletcher ,

           I wish to commission your excellent company , to manufacture for me , a plastic saw . The saw should be of pliable plastic , and should be non lethal . Pliable , soft , with pliable softness .
The construction should be of soft pliable plastic .
The saw is to be used in my act ,
"The mighty Horrendo expunges life"
To be done live on stage , the trick will be frightening in the extreme .
I have extensive experimental evidence , using recently expired animals , and a real saw . This is far too messy , and quite unsuitable for family audiences , hence my need for a less lethal saw .
The trick will be performed live on stage , in front of a large audience , I will be cutting in half , my own dog Boris .
A recent rehearsal session with our rabbit , Compost , proved to be an appalling experience for the practice audience of , my two daughters Wendy and Victoria , who witnessed the poor bunny being severed .
Boris is a fine lad , and is much loved , as you can imagine I do not wish to actually harm him . Boris is highly trained . He can feign terror , pain , and indeed death on command .
I can envisage my new act to be a real winner , and be my break into the big time , but I must not harm any living creature in my act .
Your budget is a maximum of £200 . Postage and packing negotiable .
Please do not hesitate to contact me , at the above address , with any questions or concerns you may have .
When I have made it big , be assured your company will be mentioned as a prop supplier to , "The Mighty Horrendo" .
A modest sketch of the tool would be sufficient for me to commission the works . Perhaps you could instruct the Apprentice , or a junior , to knock one up as a practice piece and then sell it on to me . Should your company be unable , or too busy , for this commission , you could , perhaps , recommend another firm .

I await sir , your reply , in your good time .

Yours most sincerely .   The Mighty Horrendo .

THERE WAS NO REPLY TO THIS LETTER .   Later that year The
Mighty Horrendo attempted an even more dangerous trick , and succeeded
in expunging this own life in hideous circumstances .
(The Mighty Horrendo)

The Chartered Institute of Waste Management .
9 Saxon Court ,
St Peter's Gardens ,
MAREFAIR ,
NORTHAMPTON .
NN1 1SX .

Mr L Poker .
Copperwalls Lodge ,
DEVON .
16 - 02 - 2010 .

Dear Sir ,

      I have , for many years , feared for our planet . My latest study paper , (there has been 19 in all) , centres on the unpalatable subject of waste , its management , use , and potential value .

Primarily , Eco Industrial Symbiosis , defined , essentially as , the sharing of information , services , utility and product resources among one , or more actors , in order to add value , and reduce costs promoting environmental improvement .

Eco - industrial development is needed on a large , and indeed urgent scale , to pioneer fully integrated industrial ecology . Such an initiative seems to be lacking , not just in the UK , but across Europe and beyond . One major advance could be achieved by creating "Recycling clusters". By means of establishing a resource exchange network , a reduction of public fear perception could be achieved at relatively low cost , allaying concern over pollution , degradation , and the depletion of natural resources .

The introduction , albeit , in my opinion , on an ad hoc basis , of the polluter pays principle , will assuage the natural public vengeance gene . Extended Hierarchy responsibility , as well as increased education , and awareness of the responsibility we all must shoulder , are essential . Promotion of "hands on" participation , by the populace , would be a massive boon , for example , Vegans could reliably called upon to contribute by supplying "envirostools". This could be collected and used as a Eco - neutral fertiliser . One of many , natural , harmless fertilisers . In conclusion , we have but one planet , one , but one , opportunity to destroy or save it . I vote to preserve rather than try to reassemble the broken parts afterwards . We must act now .

I look forward to your observations , and comments , in reply .

I have the privilege to be , and shall remain sir , your obedient servant .

Lionel Poker .

The Chartered Institution
of Wastes Management

9 Saxon Court, St Peter's Gardens, Marefair, Northampton, NN1 1SX. United Kingdom.
T: +44 (0) 1604 620426   F: +44 (0) 1604 621339   E: ciwm@ciwm.co.uk   W: www.ciwm.co.uk

Mr Lionel Poker
Copperwalls Lodge

DEVON

19.2.10

Dear Mr Poker

I read your letter of 16th February 2010 with interest and I have been asked by my colleagues to respond on behalf of the Institution.

We share your concerns regarding the need to utilise resources sustainably, raise public awareness and increase participation in waste prevention and recycling.

Waste and resource management is an issue which goes beyond the individual, Government and industry it involves us all and the action needs to be global. But all is not doom and gloom there is a lot of good work being done by for example the Environment Agencies in monitoring and enforcing waste legislation and by the Waste and Resource Action Programme (WRAP) in raising awareness of recycling and better use of resources.

Finally if I may be a little critical of one item in your letter, I do not consider that the application of human excrement to soil, no matter how eco-neutral it may be considered, beneficial in terms of health or agricultural productivity.

Yours faithfully

Chris Murphy
Deputy Chief Executive

Mr Hebridean Mutton .
10 TOLSTA CHAOLAIS,
ISLE OF LEWIS ,
SCOTLAND .
HS2 9DW .

Mellissa Mutton ,
Copperwalls Muttonlodge ,
DEVON .
23 - 09 - 2009 .

Dear Mr Hebridean Mutton ,

I have , for some time now , been trying to track down possible distant family members .

My searches have revealed very few Muttons , indeed I have yet to find another , until now it would seem . Perhaps , you are attached to the European part of the family . I do recall that in the 1920s some Muttons did resettle in France . You could be a descendent of one of the émigré Muttons . Was your father , or possibly your grandfather , a Maurice Mutton ? , or indeed , Moûton . Did you have a Margaret Mutton in the family , or perhaps a relative named Melvin ? .

My investigations have been difficult due to my own rather timid disposition . I have trouble communicating on a one to one basis , due to the high level of teasing and ribbing I endured during my early years , especially at school .

I am sure I would not have to enlarge on that to you , being a Mutton you probably had a hard time too at school .

Please help if you can and tell me if any other of us Muttons are out there that you know of . In Scotland , perhaps they are now McMutton , Having been naturalised into the Caledonian ways . Are you and your family members still keeping up the old tradition of giving all children a name beginning with M ? .

If it helps with your investigation , my Father was called Malcolm Mutton , my mother was called Clair , (she obviously married into the Muttons , maiden name Clack). My grandfather , (paternal) ,was named Martin , and had three brothers , Mark , Miles and Mortimer .

Eleven sisters called , Megan , Maureen , Matilda , Martha , Magdalene , Mabel , Myrtle , Mavis , Mary , Marigold and Melanie .

The eldest , Megan , had five sons all called Michael .

That's about all I know , I do hope you can fill in some gaps .

I hope to hear from you very soon , yours most sincerely , Mellissa .

Mellissa

The Mutton Family

10, Tolsta Chaolais

Isle of Lewis

HS2 9DW

3rd October 2009

Miss Mellissa Mutton,

Copperwalls Muttonlodge

Whitestone

Devon

EX24 2HT

Dear Mellissa,

We are all intrigued by your letter, and I have hastened to reply. My old father, Murdo Mutton , had two sayings that always amused us at family gatherings:

"We muttons try not to hang around" and

"We muttons should always hang together"

Both are applicable to the present situation.

I am surprised that you did not guess that Hebridean Mutton was a mere nickname. I, like my father and my two sons, am called Murdo Mutton, we have a very strict patronymic naming system here which explains why such nicknames are necessary.

There is nothing of the French about us, There have been Muttons on this island for as long as people can remember. Indeed this island is full of Muttons and people are often teased and ribbed at school, and even sometimes beaten to a pulp, if they are not called Mutton.

It seems to me plain that your branch must have left the Island at some distant time, perhaps to deliver meat to the starving people on the mainland. This is a traditional Mutton occupation, and before the advent of the sat.nav. there was always the risk that people would not find their way home.

I hope that this is of help in your researches, and that at some time in the future we will know what sort of Mutton you are.

Yours aye

Murdo Mutton

Murdo – for the Mutton family

Food Standards Agency.
11th Floor ,
Southgate House ,
Wood Street ,
CARDIFF CF10 1EW .

Gerald Goon-Stopford .
Copperwalls Lodge ,

DEVON .

12 - 06 - 2009 .

Dear Sir ,
     I have a health related enquiry , regarding Pork , and thought you were my best chance of a definitive answer .
You may be aware that in recent years the wild boar has made something of a comeback in the countryside hereabouts . Truly wild , the Boar families can be of two adult , (a breeding pair) , and up to 12 piglets .
Last year the pigs caused great damage to Wheat , Maize and rape crops .
A hunting party was hastily assembled , a group of affected farmers , and local gunmen went out into the woods and killed 4 of the animals . Along with the porcine fatalities , gunshot injuries were sustained to 3 of the posse , all minor , mainly superficial leg and genitalia wounds .
The second such party , last Autumn , killed 3 more pigs with no human injuries , mainly due to the hunt being conducted prior to the session in the local hostelry , rather than after . Also the ban on old and inaccurate Captain Charles Hanson , (retired) , from using his old and inaccurate Blunderbuss , a relic from a long forgotten war . (Him and his gun) .
The Piglets killed on the first hunt , were spit roasted , in the pub garden , with some diners going down with food poisoning . Although the pork was suspected , the landlord , now replaced , was found later to have provided meals to patrons which contained , among other things , mouse body fragments and pieces of torn and dirty underpants in the Irish Stew .
To return to my original enquiry , does the wild boar have any particular condition that would preclude it from being safely consumed ? .
Does the wild boar pork carry any known disease ? .
Pankhurst , (veterinarian) , (retired) , declared the pork good upon inspection . He , however , had been on the port , and approved of the contaminated stew , and indeed wanted more , when asked to opine .
In short , was it the pork or was it the pants that caused the sickness ?.
I ask , and indeed , beg your advice as the hunt is to be reassembled next month . The party this year is to be the farmers , a few Gung - ho local hot heads , a doctor , and the very reverend Bostock of Whitestone parish church . I have advised the doctor to bring his bag along in case of unforeseen injury . Hopefully with Captain Hanson now confined to his bath chair , the doctor will be required only as a killer and not a healer .

Yours in anticipation of good advice .   Goon - Stopford ,

FOOD
STANDARDS
AGENCY

Gerald Goon-Stopford

Copperwalls Lodge,

, Devon,

Friday 3 July 2009   Reference:

Dear Mr. Goon-Stopford,

Thank you for your letter dated 12 June 2009. You asked whether wild boar have any particular conditions that would prevent them from being safely consumed.

As a general background, fresh meat of any species is in itself not a sterile product as it carries on the surface micro-organisms. Some of them are spoilage bacteria and some may be food pathogens e.g. *Salmonella*. The multiplication of micro-organisms depends on the temperature of the environment, the acidity of meat, water content, nutrients and time. Subsequent unhygienic handling of meat during transport, in retail shops and in the kitchen may also affect the quality of meat and present a public health risk.

With regards to the parasites in pork meat there is no evidence from ante and post mortem inspection records kept by MHS, to suggest any worrying level of parasites in pork meat in the UK. In fact two parasites with zoonotic potential *Trichinella Spiralis (small cysts in muscles)* and *Cysticercus cellulosae (the cystic stage of human tapeworm)* have not been discovered in the UK's pork meat for decades.

INVESTOR IN PEOPLE

Room 5B, Aviation House, 125 Kingsway, London WC2B 6NH
Tel: 020 7276 8355 Fax: 020 7276 8463
E-mail: ouafa.daoudi@foodstandards.gsi.gov.uk

Managing risk from game meat begins with the individual hunter who assesses any abnormal behaviour before killing and the scope for environmental contamination as well as any abnormalities found after killing.

The majority of hunters are trained persons. This means someone with sufficient knowledge of the pathology of wild game, and of the production and handling of wild game meat after hunting, to undertake an initial examination of wild game on the spot.

To monitor Trichinella in wildlife the Agency has introduced a voluntary free Trichinella testing scheme for hunters of wild boar. All wild boars are also routinely tested for Trichinella in approved game handling establishments.

Finally, as a general advice cooking food properly will help to ensure that any harmful bacteria and parasites are killed.

I hope you find the above information useful.

Yours sincerely

Ouafa Daoudi

U.K. TAXIDERMY .
Hollydean Cottage ,
Padmans Lane ,
Boston Spa ,
West Yorkshire .
LS23 6BR .

Mr B Grillar .
Copperwalls Lodge ,
DEVON .
10 - 10 - 2010 .

Dear Sir / Madam ,

     I have long been interested in Taxidermy , and have made some crude , and indeed amateur attempts in the past .

During my 86 years on our good lords earth , I have been successful in many areas , as well as failed in equal measure .

My wish is to develop my limited abilities into something more professional . We run a smallholding here , and keep a few dozen Chickens and Ducks and , inevitably some of our flock will expire entirely naturally .

We do not run a meat operation , only eggs , and therefore never kill an animal unless it is moribund or dies due to age .

Denzil , our favourite Duck died in 2007 , I tried to preserve the boy in an amateur Taxidermical manner . I failed miserably . Some Chickens have expired in the mean time , and my stuffing attempts have been laughable .

My Granddaughters favourite Chicken , Gloria , after her unfortunate finale looked more like Denzil when stuffed . Indeed , Denzil looked like Gloria after the same treatment .

Clearly I have little natural ability in the field of Taxidermy .

Could you give me a few gems of advice .

With what sir , shall I stuff it , I have tried dried rice an that is clearly wrong , Denzil , would not remain upright . I shall not tell you how Gloria went wrong , other than polyfilla and concrete will not work .

I can confirm that the carcases were clean and empty prior to infilling .

That the birds were not left for any period of time to go off / rot .

My Granddaughter , would be delighted if the next Chicken to go could be as we say , preserved for posterity .

Kylie and Danni are looking slightly older than their human counterparts , and , should they expire prior to my families next visit , my dilemma becomes more obvious .

Kylie , a particular favourite , being the elder of the flock would probably be the next candidate .

Any tips or advice from yourselves would be most welcome .

Please do give advice , my credibility as a know all Granddad is at stake .

Yours most sincerely , with thanks in anticipation , Bert Grillar .

THERE WAS NO REPLY TO THIS LETTER .
Bert however , stuffs on regardless .
(Bert Grillar)

- 33 -

Legal Department .
SEVEN SEAS Ltd ,
Hedon Road ,
MARFLEET ,
HULL . HU9 5NJ .

Horace Sevenseas .
Copperwalls Lodge ,
DEVON .
08 - 06 - 2009 .

WITHOUT PREJUDICE .

Dear Sir ,

I note that your company is called Sevenseas . I too , sir , am sevenseas . I have been Sevenseas since 1929 . Presumably I was here first . You sir , have used my name , and I am somewhat taken aback .
Could you ,
A . Furnish me with sufficient evidence that your company is no fly - by - night outfit that might sully my , (our) , good name .
B . Assure me , that the products you manufacture , or sell , are of good quality and efficacy .
And most importantly .
C . That you did not nick my good name in 1951 after my discovery .
Please do not insult my aged , but still intact , intelligence , by claiming not to know of the well publicised formula . (The haemclaens) .
Indeed , I now live quietly in retirement , in Devon .
Not yet dead sir , I expect your reply by return , and by god sir , it better be good .

Yours Sir ,   H Sevenseas .

SEVEN SEAS LIMITED
Hedon Road, Marfleet, Hull, England HU9 5NJ.
Telephone: 01482 375234 Fax: 01482 374345

Horace Sevenseas
Copperwalls Lodge

Devon

Our ref: NGF/CAG

18th June 2009

Dear Mr Sevenseas

Thank you for your letter dated 8th June 2009.

As you will no doubt be aware, the phrase "Seven Seas" (as in the idiom "Sail the Seven Seas") can refer either to a particular set of seven seas or, to a great expense of water in general.

Throughout time, people have used the phrase "Seven Seas" for different things. In medieval European literature "Seven Seas" referred to the following seas: the Persian Gulf, the Black Sea, the Caspian Sea, the Red Sea, the Mediterranean Sea, the Adriatic Sea and the Arabian Sea (which is part of the Indian Ocean).

Whilst this medieval concept had its origins in Greece and Rome, I understand that the term "Seven Seas" has existed much longer, appearing as early as 2,300 BC in Hymn 8 of the Sumerian Enheduanna to the Goddess Inanna. Therefore, whilst it appears that you were born before this Company was incorporated, our use of the name Seven Seas refers to nautical matters, as opposed to your surname. Indeed, this Company's very existence derives from fish oil, in particular Cod Liver Oil, which by its nature is inextricably linked to the sea.

I, therefore, cannot envisage any situation in which we may have be deemed to have stolen your name. I do take this opportunity, however, to confirm that this Company is a very reputable company which produces high quality products manufactured and packed to the very strict standards required by Pharmaceutical Good Manufacturing Practice. In such circumstances, I see no reason why any association with this Company, albeit accidental, would do anything other than enhance your own reputation.

I trust this clarifies matters.

Yours sincerely
SEVEN SEAS LIMITED

Nick Fraser, Solicitor
Nick Fraser, Solicitor
Company Secretary

The Functions Manager .
BURGE ISLAND HOTEL ,
Bigbury - on - Sea ,
South Devon ,
TQ7 4BG .

Kevin Common .
Copperwalls Lodge ,
DEVON .
30 - 12 - 2009 .

Dear Sir ,
    I am writing to enquire about prices and availability to hold a function at your hotel .
My partner Sharron , and her daughter Keeley , both share the same birthday , the 29th of March . My treat to them is to pay for a big do , as both have landmark birthdays in 2010 , Sharron celebrating her 30th , and our Keeley has her 16th on the same day .
I saw your hotel on that morning show , where they took the mick out of fat people , with Loraine Kelly , it was on just before Jeremy Kyle , so we couldn't miss it really .
Keeley is not "my" daughter , but I treat her as if she were my own , her true father went back to Trinidad soon after she was born .
Not even Sharron keeps in touch with him now .
I can assure you that cost is no problem , we had a bit of a lottery win a couple of years ago , and we are well fixed . I would be spending quite a few quid , as I intend to have chicken legs , prawns , sausage rolls , aperitif's , profiteroles the lot , as well as Champers and a load of booze . Could be a right decent wage for your place .
Do you do a theme night ? , a sort of , come dressed up night ?
Sharron and Keels , both love Shell suits , and have dozens . Even I have a few . We thought , pink shell suits , (but pink track suits would do obviously) .
Being sociable people , I would be honoured and delighted if your other guests joined in if they fancied it , at no cost to them , they would be OUR guests .
I have got to say , to be fair , I am writing to another place , to get info and prices and that , so this is not a firm order yet . But , I quite fancy your place , and as long as Shaz and Keels agree , you get the gig .
I'll bung the staff a folding gratuity in the normal manner , and it wont be a fiver , I tip large .
I look forward to your reply , with the Portfolio and Manifesto etc , and price list .

Yours Sincerely , Kevin Common .

BURGH ISLAND

31st December 2009

Dear Kevin

I hope that you don't mind my calling you by your first name; while we are, I assure you, a smart and classy establishment, we are not at all stuffy and prefer a personal approach.

I see that you are fairly local to this area. Why don't you, Sharron and Keeley come for a meeting at some point with one of our Managers (Ann usually deals with our party bookings and special celebrations but any of our Managers would be pleased to meet you). We could then show you around the hotel and explain what we can offer your family and what would make your stay really special.

Pink is a very "deco" colour – think of Schiaparelli! Sharron and Keeley are obviously channeling good taste.

You will find further details about our parties at http://burghisland.com/pdf_downloads/BI_Parties.pdf, if you have access to the net – if not, we can give you further details when we meet.

Please do call and make an appointment. By the way, your name seems strangely familiar. I guess that I recall your amazing lottery win in 2007! How lovely that you are enjoying your success with Lady Luck and spreading your good fortune in such a fabulous way.

Yours sincerely

Dee Dee von Flusterbuget

Burgh Island Limited, Bigbury-on-Sea, South Devon TQ7 4BG

Company registration number: 4219765

Tel: 01548 810 514   Fax: 01548 810 243

Email: reception@burghisland.com   Website: burghisland.com

Human Resources .
PUKKA PIES LTD ,
The Halfcroft ,
SYSTON ,
LEICESTER .
LE7 1LD .

Mr W Bunter .
Copperwalls Lodge ,
DEVON .
21 - 06 - 2009 .

Dear Sir ,
      I have enjoyed your products for many years . The range of
Pies , Pasties , and savouries that your company produces are excellent .
Doubtless you are constantly trying new lines and making pies with new
and interesting fillings .

May I therefore suggest that you will be needing a pie eating expert to test
the new flavours . To Whit - my good self . I , sir , am a pie eating
expert . The phrase , "who ate all the pies" , was made for me .

I possess unique pie eating attributes .   I am a weighty individual of
some 24 stones with a very low centre of gravity , and have an extremely
discerning palate , being able to detect the presence of meat ingredients ,
and indeed , their quantities .

My current pie consumption is impressive , already large and varied , and
I intend that it should increase still further , due to my cutting out bread ,
potatoes , and fizzy drinks from my diet .

I am prepared to offer my services to your company at a realistic rate of
remuneration . I am prepared to work 5 days a week , and can test / taste
pies at a quick , and indeed alarming rate . Few , if any other tasters can
match my rate of consumption ,   I can , in fact , eat over 20 pies in one
day .

Therefore , a testing session in the morning , of say , 6 pies , could be
followed by the same at midday , and be followed by a session of equal
length in the afternoon . Can your current tasters compete with that ?,
I think not sir . As for the distance between your factory , and my home in
Devon , I have the agreement of my good lady wife who , has agreed to
take me to Leicestershire early on Mondays in our truck , and to collect me
after work on Friday afternoon , spending the week with her delightful
sister in Shirebrook .

Needless to say , I would probably not use the staff canteen at lunchtimes
very often , as my tasting duties would serve to provide most of my
necessary sustenance . I do hope that you will take up my offer of
expertise , and both parties can develop greatness in , similar , but very
different ways .

Yours Most Sincerely .   Mr W Bunter .

...don't compromise

Pukka Pies Limited • The Halfcroft • Syston • Leicester LE7 1LD
Tel: (sales) 0116 260 9755 & 0116 260 7985 • Tel: (admin) 0116 264 4004 • Fax: 0116 264 0092 • www.pukkapies.co.uk

Mr W Bunter
Copper Lodge

Devon

23rd June 2009

Dear Mr Bunter,

My brother and I enjoyed reading your letter giving the start to our day a twist of good humour.

We are both remarkably slim, love eating pies and look like we might live a long time. So, I am afraid there is not much chance of a vacancy.

In the meantime, enjoy tasting our pies in Devon and thank you for your complimentary letter.

Yours sincerely,

T D Storer
Managing Director

Directors: T. K. Storer (Chairman & Secretary)   A. J. Storer (Joint Managing)   T. D. Storer BSc (Hons) (Joint Managing)   V. C. Storer

The Dog's Trust .
17 Wakley Street ,
LONDON .
EC1V 7RQ .

Mr Piers Belton - Snooty .
Copperwalls Lodge ,
DEVON .

16 - 03 - 2009 .

Dear Sir / Madam ,

          I own the finest dog in Britain bar none . Boris , a 9 month old Collie , is as a human .

Permit me to convince you of my claim .

Boris has been tested thus , I cooked 48 pork sausages and placed them around the kitchen , in bowls , on worktops , in accessible positions , then left Boris alone in there with the sausages commanding him to leave them uneaten . I left the room , closing the kitchen door , leaving him and the sausages alone .

I returned 45 minutes later , all 48 sausages were accounted for , I congratulated Boris on his restraint .

Boris was then challenged with being placed into an enclosure with a litter of 6 small baby bunnies , he was instructed to desist from murdering them . The bunnies all survived without harm .

His next task was to retrieve a cooked lamb chop from the kitchen worktop , and deliver it to me in the living room , without consuming it on the way . Again he succeeded .

On the back of such great success , I gave Boris the ultimate challenge . To encounter , and befriend , "Bulldog" the large and fearsome farm cat .

"Bulldog" , has never , but never been handled . He kills all mice , rats , rabbits and even other cats that he encounters . He once even attacked Mr Palmer , the farmer , who still fears him .

My instructions to Boris were to walk past Bulldog , with his tail in the air iin his most nonchalant manner , and not look at him , indeed to ignore the cat .

Boris passed this test with style , as he has passed all other tests .

Boris can walk on hind legs , standing upright , and on his forelegs with hindparts aloft . On a recent training session , where next doors dog was instructed to jump through hoops that were ablaze , Boris was instructed to operate the fire extinguisher to put out the flames .

I have yet to find an assignment that Boris cannot accomplish . He is a fine dog indeed .

Do you have evidence of more accomplished dogs ? I look forward to your reply .

Yours

Piers Belton - Snooty .

Mr Piers Belton – Snooty
Copperwalls Lodge

Devon

Dear Piers,

Thank you so much for your thoroughly enjoyable letter. You must have worked very hard training him, I'm sure it has been rewarding for the both of you.

We appreciate you taking the time to write to Wag! unfortunately we are unable to print your letter due to the large amount of news stories we have received.

I do hope Boris' friendship with Bulldog the fearsome cat continues to blossom, he sounds like a very brave dog!

Thank you again for contacting Wag! Regards

Deana Selby

Deana Selby

Dogs Trust
17 Wakley Street
London EC1V 7RQ

T 020 7837 0006
F 020 7833 2701
www.dogstrust.org.uk

Patron: Her Majesty The Queen
President: The Marchioness of Northampton
Chairman: Mr PG Daubeny Honorary Treasurer: Mr S Langton FCA Chief Executive: Mrs CM Baldwin OBE
Registered Charity Numbers: 227523 & SC037843

A dog is for life, not just for Christmas®

Customer Contact Unit .
DEFRA ,
Eastbury House ,
30 - 34 Albert Embankment ,
LONDON SE1 7TL .

Mr Richard Dangle .
Copperwalls Lodge ,
DEVON .
10 - 03 - 2009 .

Dear Sir ,
    I am well over 90 years old and owe much of my longevity ,
and continued vigour , to having consumed oily fish all of my life .
Kippers have , for more than 7 decades , have been my favourite food .
Indeed , my children , grandchildren , and now great grandchildren , have
all been the fortunate beneficiaries of my only joke .

"I have 22 more bones in my body than you have" , "how granddad" ,
"I had a kipper for breakfast" .

This hilarious , and indeed , ancient joke brings me to the point of my
enquiry to you .
How is it , that in these days of genetic intervention , we have yet to
produce a boneless herring .   Breeding , and indeed , scientific methods
could surely be brought to bear by the clever bods to achieve this .
Boneless fish would , of course , be utopia as we could eat all of the fish ,
bar head and tail , no filleting required . No waste .
In a little over 4 years I shall be expecting my telegram from her gracious
Majesty .
I do hope I shall enjoy a boneless kipper before that honour reaches me .

Live long , eat fish , carry on the good work .

R Dangle .

CCU 7th Floor
Eastbury House
30-34 Albert Embankment
London
SE1 7TL

Department for Environment
Food and Rural Affairs

Email: ccu.correspondence@defra.gsi.gov.uk
Website: www.defra.gov.uk

Mr R Dangle
Copperwalls Lodge

Devon

CCU Ref: DWO125699

20 March 2009

Dear Mr Dangle,

Boneless herrings

Thank you for your letter of 10 March about boneless herrings. I have been asked to reply.

We enjoyed reading your letter and the interesting suggestion to create boneless herrings. However, I must report that there are no plans to undertake the genetic modification of herrings at present.

We do hope that this will not dampen your spirits in your approach to receiving a telegram from the Queen.

Yours sincerely,

Rachel Hopping
Defra - Customer Contact Unit

- 43 -

Archie Lawrie .
The Scottish Society
For Psychic Research ,
5 Church Wynd ,
Kingskettle ,
By Cupar ,
FIFE KY15 7PS .

Stanley Coot .
Copperwalls Lodge ,
DEVON .
28 - 01 - 2010

Dear Mr Lawrie ,
        Why sir , do I trouble to write to you , this letter .

Am I crazy ?

Yours , Coot .

"KETTLEHOLM",
5 CHURCH WYND,
KINGSKETTLE,
BY CUPAR,
FIFE.
KY15 7PS

TEL. 01337 830387
FAX. 01337 830387

Mr Stanley Coot,
Copperwalls Lodge,

DEVON.

e-mail: archie.lawrie@ukgateway.net

Feb. 10th 2010

My Dear Coot!

I should imagine that in writing your somewhat unusual letter you were attempting to "test" me in some way.
I think the following might surprise you:-

Merely by touching your letter and running a fingertip over your signature we can tell the following things about you,

a) You are a lover of classical music.
b) You have many books in your possession
c) Most of those books deal with "knowledge" of some sort.
d) You are a "wise" man as well as one with accrued knowledge.
e) You are (were) "strong". In body or in mind ??
f) You are an "obstinate" person apparently, with strong ideas.
g) You are sensitive to the spirit world.
h) You hear spirit in your property
i) And you have seen spirit fleetingly too, I think.
j) You like whisky. (More than is good for you??)
k) You talk to yourself quite a bit.
l) And lastly …and I love this bit… the word "HOOT" is closely connected to you in some way. Was it a childhood nickname perhaps?
    I just don't know but someone uses that name for you regularly.

The process that was used to obtain this information is called "psychometry"…but there again, you probably knew that already.

Should you wish to know more of the psychic world then I have written a series of books on actual cases in Central Scotland 1999 to 2009.
"The Psychic Investigators Casebook" Volumes 1, 2 and 3.

£15 each incl. P+P or £40 the set.

Your Archd. A. Lawrie
Pres. Edinburgh Socy. for Psychical Research

"KETTLEHOLM",
5 CHURCH WYND,
KINGSKETTLE,
BY CUPAR,
FIFE.
KY15 7PS

TEL. 01337 830387
FAX. 01337 830387

Mr Stanley Coot,
Copperwalls Lodge,

DEVON.

e-mail: archie.lawrie@ukgateway.net

Feb. 28th 2010

My Dear Coot!

What irks you?

I note that you do not reply to my reply to your mysterious letter.

Was I too near the truth? Has it frightened you off? …Or are you unwell?

Yours,

Arh. A. Lawrie

Archibald A. Lawrie

Archie Lawrie .
The Scottish Society
For Psychic Research ,
5 Church Wynd ,
Kingskettle ,
By Cupar ,
FIFE KY15 7PS .

Stanley Coot .
Copperwalls Cootlodge ,
DEVON .
03 - 03 - 2010 .

My Dear Lawrie ,

I admit to being somewhat taken aback by your second letter , having just stopped reeling from the content of the first . Although unnecessary , I will answer the three enquiries you put ,
a) "were you too near the truth" …….. you were .
b) "has it frightened me off" …….. no sir , why would a person who you correctly predicted as "strong in body or in mind" . fear any mortal ?
c) "am I unwell" ………. I am not .
Of the 12 predictions listed in your first letter , you score 11 , the suggestion that I drink rather too much whisky than is good for me is nothing less than a slur , I drink Port , (a little more perhaps than is good for me) .
I was , as you point out , called Hoot at school , and yes I have a great many books , and they do indeed deal with knowledge .
In replying to my original brief enquiry letter , I had rather hoped that you would make all manner of wild and inaccurate predictions , you did not . I found this a little disappointing , having just looked up the word "charlatan" , I have been itching to call somebody it , but you have an eerie accuracy about the words you use to describe me . And to cap it all you have written books and probably have letters after your name .
My love of classical music , (as you correctly deduced) , is my great comfort in life . Many an evening is spent in quiet reflection , imbibing port listening to Beethoven , Handel or the Rubettes .
Relaxation , as I am sure you will agree , is essential for inner peace . Port is less important .
I live in a house that is over 150 years old and the occasional creek , knock or thing that goes bump in the night does happen , and one time I saw an apparition . (Or does one have an apparition) . I thought I saw my long deceased Father standing at the foot of my bed in the dead of night . When I rubbed my eyes , and focussed more clearly , I could see for certain that it wasn't him . My Father was a much taller man .

Yours Sir ,

Coot .

The Chief Dentist .
British Dental Association ,
64 Wimpole Street ,
LONDON W1G 8YS .

Stanley Kevin Beefer .
Copperwalls Lodge ,

DEVON
12 - 03 - 2009 .

Dear CHIEF DENTIST ,

My name is Stanley , I am   nearly 9.
My dad says if I eat a lot of sweets my teeth will all fall out .
My dad says if I don't eat veg I will get spots .
My dad says if I eat carrots iwill see in the dark .
My dad says if I watch too much television my eyes will go square .
I don't expect you to answer all of the questions , I will write to other
experts about them . BUT , is he right about the teeth falling out ,
because I have loads of teeth , and they are all nice and white .
My mum , eats chocolate after we go to bed , I know this , I have seen it .
She still has teeth and she is very old , more than 40.
My dad has funny teeth so what does he know .
I have decided to ask the very top man in the country . YOU .
Will you tell me , as well , is only Gordon Brown higher than you in
dentist things .

Stanley kevin Beefer

Yours sincerely   STANLEY KEVIN BEEFER .

URGENT
Private and Confidential
Stanley Kevin Beefer
Copperwalls Lodge

DEVON

British Dental Association
64 Wimpole Street
London
W1G 8YS
Tel (switchboard):   020 7935 0875
Tel (direct line):   020 7563 4187
Fax: 020 7563 4554
www.bda.org

20 March 2009

Dear Stanley,

Many thanks for writing to me. What a very wise Dad you've got! He clearly knows a lot about a lot of things – He sounds to me like someone you should listen to.

As you say, I am not the one to ask about the spots and the square eyes and so on, but I will comment on what he says about your teeth.

What he says about sweets is certainly worth listening to. The sugar in sweets can cause them to get holes in and can mean you may need to have fillings or even lose teeth altogether. So it's really important that you are very careful about eating sweets and other sugary foods. You should really keep them as special treats and not have too many or have them too often.

The other thing to be careful about is to make sure you clean your teeth properly and regularly. I have put some information sheets in with this letter so that you can read up a bit more and be even more expert than your Dad. If you're on the internet you could also look at this website **http://www.dentalhealth.org.uk/** that will give you lots of interesting information about how to keep your mouth healthy. It might also be interesting for old people as well!

Gordon Brown is obviously very, very important and I'm sure he might be able to give you even more advice.

It's really good of you to write – I hope this helps in your quest to find the truth.

Best wishes

Peter Ward
Chief Executive
British Dental Association

from the office of the
Chief Executive

- 49 -

ELITE TITLES .
103 Queen Street ,
Newton Abbot ,
DEVON ,
TQ12 2BG .

GARY GOON .
Copperwalls Lodge
DEVON .
05 - 08 - 2009 .

Dear Sir ,

      I am interested in buying a Lordship . I was given your name by a good mate of mine , and thought I would give you a shout , seeing as your firm has a Titles to knock out reasonable .

I got a posh address , but I am a working class geezer , but I reckon I'm as good as the rest of them . There are a few hoity toity types round here who think I'm a bit rough , but I drive a Merc , and some of them have dirty old Land rovers . I quite fancy being "Lord Goon of Devon" or has that one already gone ? I would pay a quite few quid for that if its available . I aint interested in a Baron or a Earl , but would settle for a Sir Gary at a pinch .

At the same time , the misses would like to be Lady Goon , or does that come automatic like . And if I am a Lord , what do the kids get called ?. Our Chantelle , and our Kylie would want a title as well . Give us a price for the Lordship , and one for the wife , and a couple of small titles for ones offspringers .

Don't get me wrong son , I have plenty of the folding to pay for all this , just let me know the price , OK !

We got a big Pig and Chicken business here that makes plenty .

I intend to be a Lordship farmer , and a fancy name would get the old ball rolling nicely , so let me know what you got in stock .

Yours sincerely   Gary Goon .

Marketing and Business Consultants

MBC - 103 Queen Street - Newton Abbot - Devon - TQ12 2BG - U.K.   U.K. Tel/Fax: 0207 681 2811
email: post@mbc90.com   International Tel/Fax: + 44 207 681 2811

Gary Goon
Copperwalls Lodge

Devon

"mbc – serving clients in the global village since 1990"

10 August 2009

Dear Gary

<u>RE: Titles</u>

Thank you for your letter. Please find enclosed our brochure for your perusal.

Lord Goon of Devon would be a Seated Title and is available (Fee £995 and can include your wife). It is not custom for the children to have a Title but if you really wanted them to take a Title then Lady would apply. We will include these within the fee. Just supply their full names with your application.

I look forward to receiving your application.

Yours faithfully

For MBC

Encs.

Marketing and Business Consultants

MBC - 103 Queen Street - Newton Abbot - Devon - TQ12 2BG - U.K.
email: post@mbc90.com

U.K. Tel/Fax: 0207 681 2811
International Tel/Fax: + 44 207 681 2811

"mbc - serving clients in the global village since 1990"

Gary Goon
Copperwalls Lodge

Devon

10 August 2009

Seated Titles Available
updated 6 August 2009

Lord & Lady of "Yourtown"
Earl and Countess of "Yourtown", etc...

*Note that in addition to the examples of land parcels listed below Lady Sarah also has a small number of, as yet, un-named areas of land to which you could give your own name if you so wish. You might therefore become Lord and Lady (or Earl and Countess, etc) of your own particular place name - your own hometown for example or your place of birth.

Should this be the case simply enter the name of your choice when completing the Application for Title form - we will write to you within 14 days of receiving your application confirming your choice.

All Seated Titles are £995

Lord & Lady of Braehead	Lord & Lady of Wretton
Lord & Lady of Pertenhall	Lord & Lady of Salem
Lord & Lady of Leybourne	Lord & Lady of Hamerton
Lord & Lady of Elland	Lord & Lady of Nutley
Lord & Lady of Stanton Long	Lord & Lady of Neap
Lord & Lady of Cudworth	Lord & Lady of Stoke
Lord & Lady of Johnstown	Lord & Lady of Uphall
Lord & Lady of Naunton	Lord & Lady of Aldfield
Lord & Lady of Kimcote	Lord & Lady of "any place name"

All land parcels are insignificant in size at just
20cm x 20cm (approx 8ins x 8ins)
www.elitetitles.co.uk/seated

SPAM .
TULIP LTD ,
Seton House ,
Gallows Hill ,
WARWICK CV34 6DA ..

Charles Huggins - Drake .
Copperwalls Lodge ,
DEVON .
08 - 07 - 2010 .

Dear Customer Service ,

By Jingo , I love your product , I have been eating SPAM for over 60 years .

During the war of course , your product was a staple , yet a luxury also . Spam is excellent . I eat it twice a week , both as a main meal , and as a breakfast every Saturday morning with two of my own hens eggs .

I am nearing my 91st birthday and a great advert for Spam . I remain fit and healthy , and still wrestle , albeit now only with my dog who is under instructions not to kill .

After much soul searching and thought , I have decided to give to you , at no cost to yourselves , my latest and indeed greatest product idea .

It is , I suggest , SPEEL .

It is basically eel , but , a great twist for sales and novelty purposes the eel is packaged in a tin . Not any old tin , but a metre long tin .

Yes , a whole eel in a tin , packaged in its elongated form . ... Brilliant ? .

The product , an eel , is cooked , sliced and ready for the table , in a great big long tin , what could simpler .

A large family , or indeed a gathering of family and friends , perhaps a wedding or barbecue could all enjoy several slices each .

It would be ready sliced in the tin , and eaten straight from the tin hot or cold , or conversely , heated up with onions or condiments .

The SPEEL could be already jellied in the tin to accommodate our cockney friends , or used as a starter or speciality for those who do not eat eels as a matter of habit .

Please let me know what you think of the idea .

If the product takes off and sells millions per week , good luck , I will accept a bottle of vintage Port as royalty .

Yours most sincerely , and the very best of good fortune to you .

Charles Huggins - Drake .

THERE WAS NO REPLY TO THIS LETTER . Old Huggins Drake
continues in good health and eats Spam daily .
(Charles Huggins Drake)

- 53 -

The British Rabbit Council .
Purefoy House ,
7 Kirkgate House ,
NEWARK ,
NOTTS NG24 1AD .

Clarissa Farnsworth - Hume .
Copperwalls Lodge ,

DEVON
13 - 03 - 2009 .

Dear Sir or Madam ,

Good Morning , my name is Clarissa , I am nearing 8 years old .

I have some rabbits . My favourite is Compost , a fine and handsome Blue Rex . He is not in a club or in a society or in a breeding arrangement . He is a young bunny of 7 months and 23 days old as of this date . He is very good looking . I do understand about breeding arrangements , and will , in the fullness of time make an arrangement for him . Such arrangements are difficult and would like to ask your expert advice about his arrangement . Should I arrange for him to visit a local bunny . Or should I arrange a total stranger to do this . I will arrange this but should the bunny , (girl) , be a strange bunny ?

I know that any such arrangements are crucial , and the correct arrangement is vital .

My father seems totally indifferent to my enquiry about this arrangement. He seems not to care . These delicate arrangements have to be carefully considered , as my mother says , ill conceived arrangements could be disastrous .

Your advice would be greatly appreciated , particularly about possible breeding arrangements .

Clarissa

Yours most sincerely   Clarissa Farnsworth Hume .

Purefoy House
7 Kirkgate
Newark
Notts. NG24 1AD

Tel: 01636 676042
Fax: 01636 611683
email: info@thebrc.org
web site: www.thebrc.org

Secretary: Mrs. Jo Jalland

20th March 2009

Miss C Fransworth-Hume
Copperwalls Lodge

Devon

Dear Miss Farnsworth-Hume

Thank you for your letter dated 13th March 2009.

Your mother is right; you should take care when breeding a pure bred for the first time.

Mrs Y Hobbs-Fothergill is a District Adviser and breeds Angora Rabbits. Her telephone number is 01626 777997 and she would be able to advise you. Mr Trute was the President of the BRC in 2007, his telephone number is 01271 371783, also a District Adviser. Both of these people have been in the Fancy a very long time and also judge at shows up and down the country, they both live in or around your area.

There is an Area Specialist Club called the Southern & South Western Rex Rabbit Club, Mr A Buller is the Secretary and his telephone number is 01297 23370, he would be able to advise you also, this club covers your area.

Please look at our website www.thebrc.org there is a Junior Section that you may find very interesting.

I'm enclosing our "Starter Pack" that you might find useful.

Good luck.

Yours sincerely

Susan Mason
BC Secretary

Encls

THE PIRATE SOCIETY .   Billy Braithwaite .
92A HIGH STREET ,   Copperwalls Lodge ,
BERKHAMPSTEAD ,
HERTFORDSHIRE .   DEVON
HP4 2BL .   13-01-2009 .

Hello Sir ,
          My name is Billy Braithwaite , I loved Pirates of the
Caribbean , it was smashing.   How can I be a pirate ???   Some real
pirate s have been about only a few weeks ago . They held up a ship on
the high seas .

Jonny Dapp was great ,   I want to be a pirate , I am 8 .
I have a plastic sword and I will get a real one if my mum allows it . MY
dad recons if I become a pirate he gets 10 per cent . HE says it ewill
make HIM rich , so if he gets 10 per cent .   I will be super rich .
TELL ME How to be a pirate . I wont tell anyone else .

I BET you are called EMILY   OR   jane

Thank you   BILLY

yours ~~Fay~~ FaithLy
        BiLLy

- 56 -

The Parrot Society UK
(Registered as a Charity 268726, under the Charities Act 1960)

Billy Braithwaite
Copperwalls Lodge

Devon

20th January 2009

Dear Billy,

Thank you for your letter of 13th January.

We are however The Parrot Society not The Pirate Society but I can well understand your mistake, the words Parrot and Pirate do look very similar. Also quite a few pirates do have parrots on their shoulders in the films that I have seen.

I am pleased that you enjoyed Pirates of the Caribbean, it is a great film. I think you would be well advised to continue using your plastic sword rather than obtaining a real one, someone could easily suffer a nasty cut as real swords are really sharp.

After a search through the back issues of our monthly magazine I have come up with a picture of a pirate with a Macaw on their shoulder, please see page 216 of the enclosed magazine, I think it is the only pirate picture we have ever put in our publication.

Do continue enjoying your pirate studies.

Yours sincerely,

A Rance
Secretary

- 57 -

Waitrose Consumer advice .
WAITROSE LTD ,
Doncastle Road ,
Bracknell ,
BERKSHIRE .
RG12 1HB

Paige Turner .
Copperwalls Lodge ,

DEVON .

22 - 09 - 2009 .

Dear Waitrose ,
      My name is Paige , I am 11 , and I like tinned fish a lot .
My favourites are Tuna and Mackerel , I have even eaten some Sild , I
wonder what that is .
My question is , who kills the fishes , my Mother says that all of the fish
die quietly in their sleep , of old age , surrounded by their family and
friends . My Granddad says that all the fish are massacred in a pit by
retired madmen , who charge more than £15.00 per hour to do it .
Granddad is often wrong , Mother says he is a silly old fool , but he
knows about bombs , Winston Churchill , Bomber Harris and loads of
other things , so he might be partly right . Can you clear this up for me
please .
Anyway , fish is very good for you , and if you ever get an advert on
television , you should tell everybody that fish has Omegas in them , and
also some special oil that is very very good for you .

Yours Sincerity , Paige Turner .

Paige Turner

BY APPOINTMENT TO
HER MAJESTY THE QUEEN
GROCERS AND
WINE & SPIRIT MERCHANTS
WAITROSE LIMITED BRACKNELL

Miss P Turner
Copperwalls Lodge
Devon.

12 November 2009
1-20391924-7

Dear Miss Turner

Firstly I would like to apologise for our delay in responding to your letter dated 22 September.

I was pleased to learn that you enjoy tinned fish, especially Tuna and Mackerel.

I can assure you that our fish are killed in the most humane way. For more information, please visit our website www.waitrose.com.

Thank you for taking the time and trouble to contact us.

Yours sincerely

Parsons (Miss)
Customer Service

80 H/O

Food shops of the John Lewis Partnership

Customer Service

Bracknell, Berkshire RG12 8YA
Telephone 01344 825232
Facsimile 01344 824978

Sir Cardew Hartigan.
Copperwalls lodge,

DEVON
07-11-08

The Austin company of U.K.ltd
Cardinal point ,
Park road,
RICKMANSWORTH
HERTS WD3 1RE

Dear Sir / madam,

At long last I have found your company, bally difficult to locate.   Anyway , Charlesworth the chauffer tells me we need parts for the old A40 , my favourite , had it since 1962.   The old girl needs a front grille radiator (complete) , and an oil filter , (the overhead type), typical of the pre 1964 models.

Have the above items sent to me directly with your invoice to the above address.   Furthermore if you have the original wheel trims , and , if you keep the mahogany dashboard fascia for the 1962 , I would appreciate an estimate for the supply of same .

Expect you will   know the address of the Austin appreciation society , Austin owners club , that sort of thing , Pack the info in the jolly old parts box if can be so good .

Any tips for shifting rust from the old undercarriage wouldn't come amiss either .

Must say , the old car is a delight , and a hoot to drive , although it's a bugger in winter , cant start the old thing , bit like the old leg iron , (her ladyship) , although I shouldn't speak ill of the car should I .

Many thanks for your help in this instance .

Hartigan

CARDINAL POINT
PARK ROAD
RICKMANSWORTH
HERTS WD3 1RE
TEL: 01923 432658
FAX: 01923 432795
www.austin.co.uk

12 November 2008

Sir Cardew Hartigan
Copperwalls Lodge

Devon

Dear Sir Hartigan,

We received your letter dated 7th November 2008 but unfortunately you have contacted the wrong company.

We are The Austin Company of UK Ltd who are a Design and Construction Management Company, not The Austin car company.

We do hope you locate the right company soon and receive the parts you were after, in the meantime please feel free to peruse our latest Austin Update for 2008 and if you would like any further information on us please do not hesitate to contact us.

Yours faithfully

Prakash Davda
Managing Director

Encs

BEN BUTTER,
Coperwalls lodge,

KIT KAT
YORK
YO91 1XY

DEVON
15-08-2008

Mr KIT KAT,

My dad said that the chocholate is made first the n the wafere is put in after. Mum said that the wayfer is made fist then the choc goes on . Who is right , who is wrong ???
I am 9 , and have a good idea who is right .

Mum is usually right because she is more clever than my dad , my dad is not thick , but mum is cleverest . Our dog BORIS is of the opinion that he doesent care if its choc then wafer , or the other way round. He seems to be swayed by my dads view or my mother , deepend s who has the kit kat.
My dad said he was going to call me BREAD when I was born , and geuess whot ? They call me that at school now , Bread Butters , ha ha ha . We have a lad at our school called Boris , ha ha ha ha aha. (my dog) ... One of the lads is called . Boris ...
My dad thinks that you were called Round trees when he was a boy . ..
That was about 1975 . You probly don't have records that far back . But hes probly wrong He is now saying from the sitting room that it was terry.
Make your mind up daddy . He always says say dad not daddy . Mum quite likes him anyway , I think , mum says she has more GEC s THAN MY DAD . Dad says that he dosent need em . He works for the gas . Anyhow who is it , mum or dad ?
We moved to devon from YORKshire because my dad got a job on the gas . They talk funny here , but its still ENGLIsh

Yours most sincerely   BEN

ben

Nestlé UK Ltd

YORK YO91 1XY

Telephone   01904 604604
Faxsimile   01904 604534

Master Ben Butter
Copperwalls Lodge

DIRECT LINE: 0800 000030

DATE

DIRECT FAX: 01904 603461

002256625A

18 November 2008

Dear Master Butter

Thank you for getting in touch about Kit Kat.

We are pleased to hear that you are interested to know how these bars are made. The wafer is placed into a liquid chocolate mould. The machine sometimes jams and we miss a centre so the whole mould fills up with chocolate. If this happens, we try to reject all the solid bars but, very occasionally, one will slip through. This would mean that your mum was right Ben

We take great pride in producing really good products and can assure you our quality standards have not changed. We work hard to prevent problems like this happening so that your Kit Kat break can be as enjoyable as possible.

Thank you once again for taking the trouble to contact us.

Yours sincerely

Janet Pipes
Consumer Relations Executive
Consumer Services

The British Egg Information Service .
52A CROMWELL ROAD ,
LONDON SW7 5BE .

Mr D F Chackertat.
Copperwalls Lodge ,
DEVON .
15 - 12 - 2008 .

Dear sir ,

    I have a small flock of Isa Warren hens . They are extremely productive layers , some 0.892 eggs , per bird , per day over a one year period . They are free range and are given a varied and interesting diet . They have over an acre of ground to forage and live in . Indeed they have often got through the garden fence and added some 40 other acres of neighbouring farmland to their territory on occasions . They are now very secure in the garden . Some months ago , acting on hearsay evidence gained from fellow drinkers at the Dog and Duck in the village,   I fed the hens a little curry and the resultant eggs a few days later had the hint of the east about the taste .   The talk now in the pub is all about
"a scotch egg" . How much , say , scotch whisky could be safely given to an adult hen ?. Whisky flavoured eggs would go down a storm at the Dog and Duck . I normally sell the eggs , (unflavoured) , to my work colleagues for £1 per half dozen . The Dog and Duck lot have offered a pound per unit for boozy eggs . I have so far not fed my hens anything that would ever be considered , even remotely harmful , I would never harm my birds . We have never eaten a chicken from our flock , and nor will we , when they stop laying they will remain here in retirement for life . Also is it wrong to feed the hens bacon . The resultant flavour would have obvious attractions for breakfast .
I would very much appreciate any advice , or information , in relation to my enquiries .

Yours sincerely Don Chackertat.

Don Chackertat

- 64 -

British Egg Information Service

Mr D F Chackertat
Copperwalls Lodge

Devon

24 December 2008

Dear Mr Chackertat

Thank you for your recent letter.

It is true that the flavour and the colour of an egg can be dictated by what you feed to your hens. However, the British Egg Information Service cannot condone giving hens whisky.

As an alternative, perhaps you could wait until the patrons of the Dog and Duck have had a few too many Scotches and then surely they wouldn't recognise the difference?

Yours sincerely

Kevin Coles

Cheap Rope .
Fleet House ,
Upnor Road ,
Lower Upnor ,
Nr Rochester ,
Kent ME2 4UP .

The Magnificent Dennis Chopcock .
Copperwalls Lodge ,
DEVON
19 - 02 - 2009 .

Dear Sir or Madam ,

Please be so good as to send to me £5.00 worth of magicians rope , accompanied by an invoice for same, to the above address .
I am on a strict budget and require exactly £5 worth in value .

If there is a colour preference , I select green , if not blue , failing that , Yellow , Red or Orange .
I will not accept white rope .
Do not insult me by sending purple rope .

My requirements are for a short piece of quality rope to complete a modest knot for stage performance purposes .

Please expedite order with the utmost haste with your invoice for same .

Yours , in anticipation , of your legendary customer service .

Chopcock the magnificent .   *Dennis*

Dennis the Magnificent
Copperwalls Lodge

Devon

Cheap Rope
Fleet House
Upnor
ME2 4UP

03.03.09

Dear Dennis (The Magnificent),

I am in receipt of your request for £5.00 worth of magicians rope and much as I would be delighted to supply you, I am afraid I cannot.

Last week, a Mr H Potter visited our warehouse in a rather jovial mood and, having purchased a quantity of White magician's rope to, as he explained it, "try out a new trick on Hermione" he promptly turned the balance of our stock into snakes.

Unfortunately, our insurers are refusing to honour our claim as the assessor they sent to inspect the damage vanished without trace. We have, however noticed that the python is looking very lumpy. As a magician, I hope you will be able to sympathise with our dilemma and I wonder if I could ask you a great favour namely; could we borrow your wand and a copy of the Snake to Rope reversal trick? We will of course pay the postage both ways and return your wand together with a selection of magicians rope of various colours with our compliments.

Yours, in anticipation of recovering our legendary customer service,

Christopher the frustrated.

Technical Dept .
CROWN PAINTS .
Paint Talk Team ,
Hollins Road ,
DARWIN BB3 0BG .

Leonard Plenk .
Copperwalls Lodge
DEVON .
08 - 03 - 2009 .

Sir ,

Through the years , paint has developed from a crude coloured pigment , into the advanced efficient age of near perfection . Your company leads the field .

One problem , however , has been ever present . A passing male canine will urinate on any painted surface , be it a lamp post , or a painted fence or door .

I have developed the answer . A gloss paint with an additive to prevent fido doing his anti social deed upon our painted surfaces . The paint , has mixed within it , pork fat .   The Pork render is mixed with the paint (oil based gloss) , and the dog will not pee on it , as he is enchanted with the smell , he associates it with food .

I have tested this mixture with my dog Boris , I have painted every other fence post in my garden with the paint , the other 50% are unpainted . The painted posts are unused , the bare posts , however , reek of piss .

Marketing of the paint could take two very separate directions . The general public , Mr do it yourself , would be keen to buy the product to keep away the unwanted staining on his fence , wall or gate .

The trade could be encouraged to buy "anti dog piss paint" as a solution to their clients problem areas .

This is a winner , are you with me on this one ? , maybe my name could be included in its launch .   "Plenks anti piss paint" perhaps .   The moderately offensive words are , of course more acceptable in this day and age . However , if you want to tone it down a bit , we could drop the piss word .

It would , naturally have to be marketed as exterior paint , as the odour in the house may offend , and it would also drive the dog crackers .

Are you in ?

In eager anticipation of your reply   Leonard Plenk

- 68 -

18 March 2009

Mr L Plenk
Copperwalls Lodge

Devon

Dear Mr Plenk

Thank you for your letter and for taking the time out to share your innovative idea with us. We are always pleased to hear from our customers and take pride in listening to and acting on their valuable feedback.

To capture their feedback we operate a forum where ideas and suggestions from internal and external sources are discussed at length and where appropriate we include the best in our future plans.

Many ideas are generated each year and there could be stiff competition, however, yours could indeed have some potential. Who knows, if successful it could indeed revolutionise the coatings market.

Once again thanks for your idea and taking an interest in the Crown Paints brands.

Yours Sincerely

Geraldine Huxley

cc   M Jepson
       B Widdop

Crown Paints Limited
PO Box 37, Crown House, Hollins Road,
Darwen, Lancashire BB3 0BG
Telephone: 01254 704951 Fax: 01254 774414

A company registered to ISO 9001

Design & Technical Department .
MERCEDES BENZ UK Ltd ,
Delaware Drive ,
Tongwell ,
Milton Keynes ,
BUCKINGHAMSHIRE . MK15 8BA .

Emeritus Prof Clement Crank .
Copperwalls Lodge ,
DEVON .
17 - 05 - 2009 .

Dear Fellow Scientist ,

               I have , for some time , been working on the
ultimate anti - theft device for use in a car .
I now have it . The device is a weight detector fitted within the drivers
seat . The device , pre set at the legal owner / users weight , recognising
the owner / user prior to any attempt to start the car .
I have called the device "The Recogniser" . An incorrectly weighted
individual , (thief or unauthorised user) , will trigger the "Recogniser" ,
linked to the ignition system , and will disable the starting mechanism
rendering the car unstealable . There is nothing new , you will say , about a
weight detector , every home has a set of scales . But , here is the twist ,
the "Recogniser" has a unique ability to detect weight distribution , spread
and shape of the object placed upon it . To Whit ! the owners buttocks .
I have tested the "Recogniser" with a correctly weighted bag of lead ,
weighing the pre - determined acceptable weight , also with two persons ,
with a combined weight of the absolute exact weight . I have also tested
the "Recogniser" with a moulded shape of my buttocks , (taken from the
originals) , inclusive of testicular indentations , then weighted with
exactly the correct weight . The ignition will fail at this test too . The
"Recogniser" demands a living human , with pulse and usual movement ,
both voluntary , and involuntary (breathing , farting etc) .
The "Recogniser" has the potential to be the ultimate male accessory in the
car , due to the "wife" being automatically debarred from driving your
pride and joy , her physical disposition being impossible to replicate as
the legitimate driver . Female buttock shape being as it is , and quite
different from the male , the lack of testicular indentation being an
insurmountable obstacle for the average woman . Besides , you don't
want the wife driving an expensive car , with Punto's being so plentiful
and cheap as they are .
We are , of course , talking of the more expensive models that would have
a "Recogniser" fitted as standard .
I look forward sir , to your reply and observations , yours most sincerely .

CLEMENT CRANK .

VED/1-1035813451

Mercedes-Benz UK Limited

A Daimler Company

1 March 2009

Emeritus Prof Clement Crank

Copperwalls Lodge

Devon

Dear Professor Crank

The Recogniser" Ultimate Anti-Theft Device

Thank you for your letter dated 8 March 2009 regarding "The Recogniser".

We take all ideas and concepts to our product design and development teams based at Daimler AG on a regular basis and consider any feedback that is received. We also track market trends to anticipate changes in consumer requirements and value the opinion of our customers, using it to influence future model development.

Our creative ideas have been passed to our Product teams who will contact you directly should they wish to take this matter further.

Thank you for taking the time to contact us and for your interest in Mercedes-Benz.

Yours sincerely

Victoria Davis

Customer Support Sales Manager

Mercedes-Benz Cars

T: 01908 301306

Leonardo de Cartwright.
Copperwalls lodge,
DEVON .
12 - 11 - 2008 .

Cadbury
PO BOX 7008,
BIRMINGHAM
B30 2PT

Dear Cadbury,

I am 8 , I love your stuff , I am at home and off school for weeks and weeks because I have broke my leg. My dad says its because I am a burk. I was swinging in the swing and fell off , I hurt my leg and its my fibea that is broken. It feels much better now than it did , I have got this big pot thing on and my mum has written on it.

I ate some of the HEROES that my dad bought when I broke it , they are smashing. My dad said that I have to break the other one before I get any more , "(HES ONLY JOKING)" but they wer e good. My sister Katie rose ate loads and she hasn't even broke anything. Apart from mums best cup thing . I hid some from Katie rose but she found some, Dad said they always do rumble us lads in the end. Girls , , I mean. or he means .

The teacher came round yesterday , because she said I was missing vital work , I pretended to be asleep .   Vital ! She didn't bring anything but a card with all the names of the kids on , the girls all wrote big, so my mates could hardly write on it . Briggsy only wrote really small. And Porky on ly said ha ha on it . This letter is the only thing im doing today . Mum says it will do as school work , because it is writing. And the computer spells everything right for me . Boris , my dog . Keeps biting my bad leg . Well the plaster thing .   Boris will have to watch it.

Everytime my dad comes in he says to Boris ,, Kill , then points at me , Boris likes me too much and ignores him.   He was at work yesterday (dad , not Boris) , and he came in and said Kill . Boris was asleep .

We have chickens in the garden , well we wouldn't have them in the house . (that is dads favourite joke) , they lay eggs every day. . Dad says that they can provide Sunday breakfast AND Sunday dinner . MUM goes mad when he says that , and he knows she will , All the chickens have names , and we do not eat them . Only the eggs …   mum calls them kylie , , byonce ,, ann Widdecombe , , gloria and some other names .

SHE Always laughs when she says the names . P.s.kylie and byonce were singers and Ann widdecombe was a cabinet . I don't know who Gloria is , or was .

Briggsy and Ronan fell off the same swing after me and broke nothing , But Charmaine cut her foot after she was pushed .

Anyway the chocs that you make are top.

DON'T LET anyone push you on a swing .   Hey … LEO

PO Box 12 Bournville
Birmingham B30 2LU

Consumer Direct Line: 0800 818181
Switchboard: 0121 458 2000
Fax: 0121 451 4297

www.cadbury.co.uk

November 2008

ter Leo De-Cartwright
nerwalls Lodge

on

Ref:- 1499676A

Leo,

k you very much for your recent letter and your kind words and views regarding Cadbury
ucts.

lways a pleasure to receive such letters and we do appreciate you taking the time and
le to put pen to paper.

e find enclosed a gift which I hope you will accept with our best wishes, and I hope you get
oon.

also enclosing some fact cards relating to the history of the Company which I hope you will
teresting.

again, thank you for contacting us.

sincerely

Costello
mer Relations Department

Heir Helmut Fokker
Copperwalls lodge
Whitestone
DEVON EX4 2HT

Masterfoods
FREEPOST
Melton mowbray
Leicestershire LE13 0BR
16 - 11 - 08

Frauline,

MY dog BORIS is good , he eat all day your "pedigree mixer".   Before this change to your goods, he ate a mix of meaty part and flak , mainly meat, some flak.   He was bad in anger and was fart bad.   Much I tried with mix of rice , pea , rusk and even spreadings of pastes. Non of the pre mentioning was a success. The dump and the smell was a poor and ranking mistake by BORIS.   He now is about your good mix and is very jolly.   Eat all .   And no smell .   I win. BORIS now is slimmer and fast,   fast as a wasp.   OH!   BORIS is sheppen dog.   (borders collie).   Pretty as a pie and not any more a "stroppy little git "   like mr parker next door was calling him until he became well again.   Parker now is a friend of boris , but I am secretly telling the boy to bite Parkers bums given the half chance. Boris and me are pals and I give him the odd sweet and a bit of my pork or a chicken end if he is a good lad, but his main dinner is your good mix with pedigree meat. He wont even look at flak now. Too posh I expect. Some advice please if you would be so delighted, Boris puts the heap in the same place all the time , the very same place !. Neatly mind you , up against Parkers fence , Parker complains, says its my fault . How the hell can it be, its Boris , not me, he thinks I am doing it. Dam silly fool. Mrs Parker smells it , I don't know why. Boris is a good lad and I wont tie him up. He isn't Houdini.   Anyway can Boris be taught to heap in another place ?   How can I tell him ?
You have scientists on your company that can solve this , you have already stopped the bad fart from Boris . How about this

With you   Helmut

MARS
petcare
uk ltd

WALTHAM-ON-THE-WOLDS
MELTON MOWBRAY
LEICESTERSHIRE
LE14 4RS
ENGLAND
T+44 (0) 1664 411111
F+44 (0) 1664 415661

Mr Helmut Fokker
Copperwalls Lodge

21 November 2008

Our Ref: 37984363

Dear Mr Fokker and Boris ☺

Heir Helmut, and young Boris,
At Mars we smile, we're pleased,
Perusing through your letter
Proud that his wind has eased.
You mentioned that he's jolly,

Been happier and fast,
Oh what a wondrous product,
Relieving Boris- heart
In hand we wish you well sir,
So much so, vouchers enclosed.

And I'll put this ink to paper,
No, each line is not well-prosed.
Dearest Boris, and his happenings,

Couldn't make us love him more,
Of course we enjoyed hearing of the grumpy man next door!

A.P.B.C. are the champions,
Please feel free to call them soon - as
Behaviour is their Forte,
Contacts are below for you:

Association of Pet Behaviour Counsellors
Telephone: 01386 751 151

Registered Number 6649984

Thank you again for your wonderful letter, and if you do need to discuss Boris toilet-training habits in the garden keep Mr Parker happier, then the APBC are who I recommend for you to contact.

Once again thank you for taking the time to contact us. As a valued consumer please find enclosed a voucher to value of £2.00 to enable you to purchase more of your favourite Mars products. Please accept this with my compliments.

Yours sincerely

Jessica Wyle
Consumer Care Team
0800 738 800

Encs: PV1(2)

Research & Development
DENNIS MOWERS ,
Ashbourne Road ,
Kirk Langley ,
DERBYSHIRE DE6 4NJ .

Bertram Fortescue-Carruthers .
Copperwalls Lodge ,
DEVON .
10 - 07 - 2010 .

Dear Sir ,

It is with great sadness that I must inform you of the death of old "Bunny" Farqueson .   Edward Bigger Partridge Farqueson .

He was 99 years of age , still strong , Opinionated and awkward right up to the last .

Old Bunny was , of course , instrumental in the development of the 16 inch and the 20 inch cutting width mowers of the mid to late fifties , those with the Villiers four stroke engine .

He worked in the development department from around 1951 to late 1955 . Bunny was adamant that in those early days a recoil rope for starting was not feasible , indeed not possible , but , of course , the recoil was developed only a year or two later .

Bunny always thought that he missed out on that one . Who did figure that problem out ? .

Bunny , Commissioned in 1941 , and perpetually in touch with his old regiment of Guards , well up until his expiry , was despatched with a full and noisy military to do at the end of last week , near his old Barracks in Guilford .

The Cannonfire rubbed out a few starlings and pigeons .

And made the local Womens institute members to drop their bloomers .

(freshly baked) . (Bunnies favourite joke) .

I would ask , that if you know any of Bunnies retired colleagues that you may be in touch with , let them know that the old bugger is brown bread .

A fine old British firm Dennis , carry on the good work .

Yours most sincerely   Berty   Fortescue Carruthers .

(THERE WAS NO REPLY TO THIS LETTER .   Bertie joined Bunny a
few months later in the great Barracks in the sky .
Bertram Fortescue Carruthers)

- 77 -

G.R. WRIGHT & SONS LTD .
Ponders end Mills .
ENFIELD .
MIDDLESEX EN3 4TG .

Mr Derek Broadbottom .
Copperwalls Lodge ,
DEVON .
01 - 12 - 2008 .

Dear sir / madam ,

I am an amateur baker of sorts . I take modest and infrequent orders for funny shaped bread .

I have baked bread in shapes of teddy bears , human figures and faces .

One recent commission for a hospital , was for a pair of lungs , a bed and a foot .

I have made animal shapes for my grandchildren .

Of late I have being taking orders for bread for stag do's , rugby club and private gatherings and the like .

You can imagine the images they demand , and indeed are prepared to pay well for .

I have baked successfully bare buttock shapes and indeed breasts .

The difficulty I have is the differing size , shape , and relative volume of bread dough contained within a set of male genitalia .

I do hope my enquiry does not cause offence .

When I have tried this recently , I get a disproportionate size and volume of the two component parts , within the three shapes that are needed .

In the process of rising / proving , I use the fireside at home .

I use oiled clingfilm to cover the bread , my late mother always used a damp tea towel .

The component parts , (of the aforementioned male genitalia) , have differing depths and volumes , so regular turning is essential .

I have ended up with a large penis , and small testicles . And vice versa on occasions .

I have found your bread mix absolutely first class for every type of bread that I make . I am determined to carry on with it .

I do hope your baking / research department can give some advice on my little problem , or should I say large problem , I believe the error I am making is in the rising process .

Your input would be very much appreciated .

Yours sincerely   Derek Broadbottom .

9th December 2008

Mr. D. Broadbottom
Copperwalls Lodge

Devon

Dear Mr. Broadbottom

Thank you for taking the trouble to write into our company in regard to moulding with our various bread mixes.

I think it maybe preferable to make a dough from scratch. This type of moulding requires a "dead" dough such as the type you use for making harvest festival plaits. I am sure you will find a recipe in one of the many bread making books available or on the internet.

Our mixes are created from a high protein content wheat flour and the physical properties of the dough from this product makes it more elastic and therefore, difficult to mould into specific shapes.

I trust this information is of use but if you are unsuccessful, please do not hesitate to contact us again. Whilst writing, may I confirm that more information will be posted to you, under separate cover, which includes a money off coupon and free recipe booklet.

Yours sincerely,

Deb the Bread
Wright's Mixes Marketing.

G.R. Wright & Sons Ltd
THE FLOUR MILLERS
Ponders End Mills, Enfield, Middlesex, EN3 4TG Tel: 020-8344 6900 Fax: 020-8804 0533
www.wrightsflour.co.uk   e-mail: sales@wrightsflour.co.uk

The Japanese Embassy ,
101 - 104 PICCADLLY ,
LONDON W1J 2JT .

Mr Kevin Carpet .
Copperwalls lodge ,
DEVON .
17 - 11 - 2008 .

Dear sir ,

My friend , and near neighbour , Mr Garratt is learning Japanese by means of private tuition . As we were both rugby players in our youth , some time ago now , I thought that a small prank could be played on him , perhaps for his birthday , which is in a few weeks time . By the way in the 1980s and 1990s , I played rugby for a side in Surrey that had an annual fixture with London Japanese . It was the favourite fixture of the season . Most of the chaps worked in the city , at the national bank , I believe . The players , who were all Japanese , were always well up for the jolly game playing in the clubhouse after the match . They were all first class chaps , and a very loyal and disciplined team . Anyway if you could perhaps let me know a few words , of say , mild derision , a modest insult perhaps , I would very much appreciate it . My friend would find it extremely funny . Maybe the words , " you silly old fool , or something similar . If I could write Japanese characters , spelling out a mild insult such as that , it would make for an excellent practical joke.
I do hope you can accommodate my odd request .

Many thanks in anticipation of your time   Kevin Carpet .

JAPAN INFORMATION AND CULTURAL CENTRE
EMBASSY OF JAPAN   LONDON

November 21, 2008

Mr. Kevin Carpet
Copperwalls Lodge

Devon

Dear Mr. Carpet,

Thank you for contacting the Embassy of Japan.

With regard to your enquiry I believe - while Japanese people are not prone to openly insulting their fellow man for fun or otherwise - the most widely known Japanese insult is "baka", which means "fool". If you want to write this on a card you can use either of the following styles:

馬鹿 or

ばか

The first in the Kanji form and the second is the Hiragana form. Depending on your friend's language level is will at the very least be able to identify and read the Hiragana form.

I hope that help you with your preparations for your friend's birthday.

Sincerely,

Grant MacKinnon

Coordinator for Public Relations
Japan Information and Cultural Centre
Tel. 020-7465-6500 (Ext.6544)

Japan-UK 150
www.uk.emb-japan.go.jp

adilly, London W1J 7JT

URL http://

馬鹿ばか

Richard Holder .
Thornton House Farm .
227 Pilling Lane ,
Preesall ,
LANCASHIRE ,
FY6 OHH .

Derek Drake . (President) .
The Devon Duck Alliance ,
Copperwalls Ducklodge ,
DEVON .
20 - 02 - 2011 .

Dear Holder ,

       Eee Baaah Gum , I have had the privilege of viewing , and enjoying , your very excellent website .

There is a good deal of important Duck related items on view .

Ducks , are my life , I love them .

I must however , turn my attentions , to acquainting you with the very serious omission on your part .

You have not , as far as I can see by your literature , affiliated your good selves with a professional trade body .

At the DDA , we offer such a service .

We naturally deal in , and with , Ducks .

The local pub for instance , will trade 8 pints of "Legtangle Cider" , per Campbell White Duck .

An Aylesbury will get you 12 pints , and so on . The local garage will service your Tractor for a small flock of 14 .

The newsagent / general store , will trade all manner of goods , such as Salt , Lard , Treacle , rennet , and liquorice for Ducks .

Basically , a Duck is worth 4 Chickens (in lay) , 6 Ducks equate to one Lamb , and a cow is negotiable . A Horse is hundreds of Ducks .

Membership to our body , The DDA , is subject to acceptance by the committee , made up of local men , Duck breeders mainly , and one woman , she is there purely for legal reasons of equality , and for making the tea .

If you choose to apply , your application will be heard by the inner Junta of the committee , chaired by my good self .

There are absolutely no benefits in joining the DDA , and absolutely no costs or obligations from members .

What say you ? Are you in , or are you on the outside of cutting edge Duck technology and development forever .

Get thee self in lad .

Yours Most sincerely , Your future President , Derek Drake

THERE WAS NO REPLY TO THIS LETTER
Derek Drake is still the dictatorial head of The Alliance .

GREEN GIANT .
General Mills UK LTD ,
PO BOX 363 ,
UXBRIDGE UB8 1YT .

ROYSTON CARRUTHERS .
Copperwalls Lodge ,
DEVON .
28 - 11 - 2008 .

Dear Jolly green giant ,

I am 9 . My brother Tarquin is 6 . He thinks
that if he eats your sweetcorn he will turn into a green giant when he
grows up .   Will you please write a letter to him and tell him it isn't true .
Eating vegetables is good for him , and for me , and for everybody . He
likes to eat them , but wont eat all of them , he thinks if he leaves a few it
wont turn him green .
He is just being a fool . I have punched him 3 times about this , and I might
punch him again , unless he stops it . Mother says I must not punch him .
So , I punch him in secret , in his room , or in the garden . He deserves it .
I am also trying to train our dog to attack Tarquin . Boris wont attack him
though . Well not really , only a bit . Boris eats the sweetcorn , but he
eats everything .
Please send a letter to Tarquin . He lives at the same address as me .
I have a sister as well .

Yours   sincerely   ROYSTON CARRUTHERS .   Royston

Green Giant®

Mr R Carruthers
Copperwalls Lodge

Devon

11th December 2008

Dear Mr Tarquin Carruthers,

Thank you for contacting us at Green Giant.

We wish to assure you that you will not grow up looking green like the Jolly Giant Giant if you eat all your vegetables.

It is very important that you eat vegetables as part of a healthy balanced diet. Current reccomendations advise that one eats at least 5 servings of fruit and vegetables per day.

Please do not hesitate to contact us if you have any more questions you wish to ask Green Giant.

Yours sincerely,

P.P.R.worrington

A. Bristow
<u>Consumer Relations</u>
Ref: 000200215884
Enc: Grow Chart

FOOD STANDARDS AGENCY
AVIATION HOUSE ,
125 KINGSWAY .
LONDON WC2B 6NH .

Dr Renfrew McTroot .
Copperwalls lodge ,
DEVON .
06 - 01 - 2009 .

Dear Sir / madam ,
        Since retiring from practice , some 22 years ago , and
having moved to the country , I have been actively conducting a rather
interesting experiment . With my large garden , I can grow all of our
vegetables for my wife Morag , and myself , also all of our meat is either a
chicken of our own flock , or   meat given , traded for vegetables , or road
kill .
Some legally hunted game , such as bunnies , pigeon , garden snails ,
frogs , toads , hare and even the large rats that are common in these here
parts .
As a retired doctor of medicine , you will imagine my butchering skills are
reasonable , and indeed I have become most proficient .
Skinning and boning a rabbit is a good deal easier than boning a rat . I
have , in fact , even tried boning a mouse . This is not worth the effort as
the meat content yielded is so small .
My reason for writing to you is to ask your advice as to what oil or fat
would be best when frying various meats . Hitherto , all frying was done
in our own dripping , collected from the roasted animals . May I not need
to mention that if you fry rabbit , in rat dripping , the tastes can
occasionally combine to produce a confusing , but interesting flavour .
Can you suggest a neutral frying medium that will not interfere with the
natural taste of the meat . I have recently acquired a portion of venison ,
The rear quarter , with a leg , the buttock and a little rib section . Traded
for cut logs / firewood .
I am looking forward with eager anticipation to trying the venison with
fresh vegetables .
As we have no license to keep a pig , and breakfast beckons , today it is
eggs from our own flock , and rat , bacon would be preferable , but unless
the wild boar come back soon , bacon is off the menu .
I look forward to your answer to my enquiry .

Yours faithfully   Dr Renfrew McTroot

FOOD
STANDARDS
AGENCY

Dr Renfrew McTroot

Copperwalls Lodge

Devon

21 January 2009   Reference: TOC02386

Dear Dr McTroot

Thank you for your enquiry which has been passed to the Nutrition Division to respond.

In regards to 'a neutral frying medium that would not interfere with the natural taste of meat' the Food Standards Agency would consider this to be a matter of personal preference. However, the Agency would recommend, as part of general healthy eating advice, olive, rapeseed, sunflower, soya bean and corn oil as healthier options for cooking, grilling and frying food as these are low in saturated fat and rich in unsaturated fats that have shown to lower blood cholesterol.

In theory, meat from road kill should be prepared in the same way as any other meat, with great care taken to avoid cross contamination and ensuring food is cooked thoroughly until piping hot throughout, reaching a core temperature of 70°C for 2 minutes. However, the Food Standard Agency would not advocate cooking and eating road-kill, and therefore cannot give more specific advice on how to best to cook it. There are various reasons for this, including the possibility that the animals you find may not have been healthy when killed and may have been suffering from

INVESTOR IN PEOPLE

Room 6b, Aviation House, 125 Kingsway, London WC2B 6NH
Tel: 020 7276 8931   Fax: 020 7276 xxxx
E-mail: samantha.montel@foodstandards.gsi.gov.uk

disease or environmental contamination which could have an adverse effect on your health.

It is also possible that an animal have been on the roadside for a long time allowing harmful level of bacteria, possibly including anaerobic bacteria such as *Clostridium botulinum* to grow. *C. botulinum* can produce a very powerful toxin that causes botulism – a severe form of food poisoning which can be fatal.

For more information please refer to our website on:

http://www.eatwell.gov.uk/keepingfoodsafe/

Yours sincerely

S Montel
Nutrition Division

The Public relations Officer .
The Geological Society ,
Burlington House ,
Piccadilly ,
LONDON W1J 0BG .

Dr Ignatius Layer .
Copperwalls Lodge ,
DEVON .
20 - 06 - 2010 .

Dear Sir or Madam ,

Rock on !

Yours sincerely   Dr Ignatius Layer

THERE WAS NO REPLY TO THIS LETTER
Dr Layer , However had good news to celebrate shortly afterwards as his
wife Sandy , gave birth to their third Child Brick . A young Brother to their
two other Children , Impervious and Sedimentary .

The British Library .
ST PANCRAS ,
96 EUSTON ROAD ,
LONDON NW1 2DB .

Henry Tudor .
Copperwalls Lodge ,

DEVON
24 - 03 - 2009 .

Dear Sir / madam ,

Hello , my name is Henry and I am nearly 10 .
My Mother , Mrs Wendy Tudor , registered my name quite soon after I
was born . This is quite normal . My father is called Henry as well , he
is called Mark as well , and Donald as well . He has 3 first manes but
only 1 last name . The whole point of this is that my mother said to me
that Granddad was called Henry as well , and some other ancestries were
called Henry as well , and I am the eighth one in our family . SO , I AM
HENRY THE EIGHTH . AND , My name is Tudor . How about that .
We have done some work on Henry the eighth at school , and he got
married six times I think . I also saw some pictures of him , but I cant
quite see what he looks like very clearly .
What I would like to ask you is , do you have any photographs of him
that you could send me . I wonder if he looks anything like me , or
maybe he looks a bit like my Granddad , because he is very old , and a bit
fat , and Henry the eighth was a bit fat .
With your computers , can you find out if I am a great , great , great
grandson of his . Or is this impossible because of lost records and things .
I will understand if you cant find these old things as it must be very
difficult to keep old things safe without tearing them .
What were his wives called , I know that 2 were called Katherine , and
one was called Jane , what were the others called ? .
Please write back soon .

henry Tudor

Thank you very much .   Henry Tudor .

THE BRITISH LIBRARY

96 Euston Road
London
NW1 2DB

T +44 (0)870 444 1500
www.bl.uk

THE WORLD'S KNOWLEDGE

Henry Tudor
Copperwalls Lodge

Devon

Ref RR 09/497/bs

27 March 2009

Dear Henry

Thank you for your letter dated 24 March.

You certainly have an interesting name – especially in this year (2009), five hundred years since Henry VIII came to the throne.

Henry died in 1547, years before the invention of photography, so you would not find a photograph of him.   There are, however, a number of paintings of him in major art galleries, perhaps the most famous being a portrait by the artist Hans Holbein the Younger in the Thyssen-Bornemisza Museum in Madrid. Do you have internet access at home or at school ? If so, I suggest you go to the web page www.museothyssen.org/thyssen_ing/coleccion/ficha713.htm where you can view this famous image (instructions to zoom etc are in English).   Henry has, of course, been depicted many times on film and TV, most recently by Jonathan Rhys Meyers in the series *The Tudors* shown on BBC within the past couple of years - for information I enclose a print of Jonathan in the role (NB this is an actor, not the king himself !).

I am afraid that the British Library would not be able to help investigate whether you are a descendant (or not) of Henry since we do not possess those kind of resources. I doubt if you would ever be able to prove or disprove the fact – there are researchers (such as the Sticks Research Agency, website www.stick.org.uk, associated with Dr Nick Barratt, website www.nickbarratt.co.uk, whom you may have seen on the TV programme *Who Do You Think You Are ?)* who **might** be able to help or advise.

For the record Henry VIII's wives were Katherine of Aragon, Anne Boleyn, Jane Seymour, Anne of Cleves, Katherine Howard and Katherine Parr.

As you may be aware, this Library is holding an exhibition about Henry to mark the 500th anniversary, details at www.bl.uk/henry

I hope this information is of help

Yours sincerely

Bart Smith

enc.

- 91 -

WALL'S SAUSAGES .
KERRY FOODS ,
Thorpe Lea Manor ,
Thorpe Lea Road ,
EGHAM ,
SURREY TW20 8HY .

Boris Beau-Walcott .
Copperwalls Lodge ,
DEVON .

05-01-2009 .

Dear Sir / madam ,
      I do hope you can help me with regard to a
competition run by your company in the mid 1950s.
My Grandfather , won the competition , and was crowned "Mr Sausages"
1956 . He was Alfred Walcott , known as "PRETTY BOY WALCOTT" .
I believe the runner up that year was Roger , or Ronald , Bone .
I can recall seeing the certificate and trophy proudly displayed on
grandpa's mantle piece in the late fifties when I was just a small boy .
My granddad died in the sixties , and , as Grandma is now also deceased ,
none of the remaining family have any record of his great victory . The
event was not a beauty contest , but a measure of health and vigour , the
contestants were fine young men in their prime , with a muscular , and fine
physique . The contest was , I believe , held in Melton Mowbray .
Grandfathers prize was fifty shillings cash , and a years supply of best
pork links .
During my Grandfathers year as reigning "Mr Sausages" , much
disapproval was expressed by my Grandmother , as Grandpa would
receive letters and cards from , as he put it , people he didn't even know .
Some of the letters would be of a suggestive and furtive nature . Indeed he
received some 13 proposals of marriage , even though already wed .
Many more proposals of , shall we say , romance , and dare I say
debauchery .
I wonder that even after this length of time , your company records still
have the result of that years contest , and if a replacement certificate could
be sent to me as a reminder of good old Pretty Boy's achievement .
There is a remote possibility that another Sausage manufacturer ran the
competition , but who else but Wall's could have the clout in the sausage
world at that time , no , surely it was Wall's .
Please do help if you can , I would love to tell "my" Grandchildren that
there was a champion in the family .
I must confess to still referring to myself as "Mr Sausages" grandson .

Yours Sincerely

Boris   Beau-Walcott

THE FINEST CUTS

www.wallssausages.co.uk

Your Reference   N/A
Our Reference   100828

Mr Boris Beau-Walcott   21 January 2009
Copperwalls Lodge

Without Prejudice

Devon

Dear Mr Beau-Walcott

Thank you for your recent letter which has been brought to my attention regarding the Mr Sausage Competition,

I have made enquires at our production site and they have unable to locate any information in their archieves with regards to this competition.

I also made contact with Unilever who used to own Walls before Kerry Foods did but sadly again they were unable to help. They did suggest you contacting your local Newspaper Agency and maybe they might be able to find something in their achieves.

My apologies for not being able to help you further.

Please find enclosed a Wall Voucher and we hope you will continue to enjoy our product.

Yours sincerely

ollaig Dunne

Consumer Relations Executive

The Head Keeper .
The Elephant house ,
Elephant . Co . ok ,
Capital Tower ,
Greyfriars Road ,
CARDIFF ,
CF10 3AZ .

Darren Daft .
Copperwalls Lodge ,
DEVON .
27 - 07 - 2009 .

Dear Mr Keeper ,

My name is Darren , I am 8 , I like elephants because they are big .

I have a lot of elephant pictures of elephants .

I have a elephant pillow and a elephant duvet .

How big is your biggest elephant what is his name how old is he and how much poo do you have to take away every day ? .

I am trying to persuade my parents to take me , and my sister , Rebecca to come to see your elephants in the summer holidays .

Dad has to get animal leave from work , he says , to do it . But he says that he will if he can .

And , do the Elephants have names ?

And , how many do you have ?

Please write back soon , I am very excited about it .

Darren

Thank you   DARREN

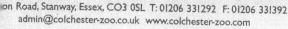

on Road, Stanway, Essex, CO3 0SL T: 01206 331292 F: 01206 331392
admin@colchester-zoo.co.uk www.colchester-zoo.com

ACTION FOR THE WILD

Dear Darren,

My name is Alison and I am a presenter at Colchester Zoo. I get to see the elephant keepers every day, and today the head elephant keeper asked me to pass on some very important information to you. He also asked me to say sorry he did not write this letter himself, but he cannot keep computers along with the elephants because the elephants can be a little heavy handed!

I'm glad to hear you like elephants; they are my favourite animals too. We have four African elephants at Colchester Zoo. Tembo is our largest elephant and he is the only boy that we have, we unfortunately do not know how old he is as he was rescued from a circus so we do not know his age. The other three; the females are Tanya who is 28, Opal who is 27 and Zola who was rescued along with Tembo. We should soon have five elephants at the zoo as Opal is pregnant; she is due to have her baby in April!!

Tembo being our largest elephant can produce up to 6 stones of poo (dung) a day. That is the same weight as the average 11-12 year old. So you can imagine the amount of poo clearing the elephant keepers have to do each day.

I hope that your Dad can get 'animal' leave and you all get a chance to come and see our elephants. Members of the public can feed Tanya at specific times, so this I can imagine you would really enjoy doing. Also at the end of each day we have an elephant training session where the keepers do health checks on the animals and this is very interesting to watch!

I hope all your questions on behalf of the head elephant keeper have been answered, however if you do have any further questions please contact us again.

Thank you for the interest in our elephants and I hope to see you soon

Kind Regards

Alison Parish

Zoo is devoted to furthering understanding of, and respect for animals. As a recognised International centre of excellence, it undertakes
n, research and education. Action for the Wild is a registered charity dedicated to assisting conservation projects worldwide.
Office as above. Registered in England No 1271226. Vat Reg No 286 1701 51
irector: DA Tropeano / Director Secretary: AK Tropeano.
he Wild is a charity registered at the Charity Commission No 1105621.
Downing, SD Knuckey, LJ Spurgeon, PR Johnson
n recycled paper

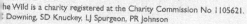

BIAZA   EAZA   BALPPA

The Honourable Secretary .
The Royal Horticultural Society ,
Vincent Square ,
LONDON .
SW1P 2PE .

Major D F Clampywick (ret) .
President .
The Devon Parsnip Alliance ,
Copperwalls Lodge ,

DEVON
27 - 07 - 2009 .

Sir / Madam ,

Permit me to introduce to you The Devon Parsnip Alliance , we are quite new , (only about 8 years in existence) , we number 56 members . A membership that is growing , just as our Parsnips are , we are all Parsnip fanatics , and in fact all growers . Myself as President , am a crusty old fart , retired , with vast pension and little else to do other than grow the next "best in show" , (hopefully a mighty beast) , and further promote the finest vegetable on our good lords earth .

Our local , (very local) , show is fiercely competitive , the largest qualifying Parsnip last year being in excess of a foot long , and weighing some three and a half pounds , a magnificent Parsnip to any eye .

Parsnips are amazing and very good for you . Naturally you would expect me to say that , and indeed , expound the virtues and versatility of the , not so , humble Parsnip . The Parsnip is a true king in the vegetable world , the recipe potentials are endless , in fact one members wife , Gloria Freewheel , Wife of last years champion , Frankie , has a myriad of ideas on how to enjoy the mighty root in ones diet .

To whit : Parsnip and Apple soup . Parsnip and Lentil soup .
Parsnip au gratin . Parsnip Julienne .
Stuffed Parsnips . Parsnip Jam . Parsnip ice cream . Parsnip Cake .
Hare and Parsnip , Parsnip and Hare , Pork and Parsnip and Cheesy Parsnips , grilled , be it with Parmesan or your local cheese .

The only two points to note with Parsnips , to the non Parsnip afficianardo are , is that they be primarily firm to the touch , and secondly they be very large . To the amateur grower , a good sized Parsnip is still a triumph , but big is best .

Your observations would be greatly appreciated , and indeed your letter , in return to mine , would be read to our assembled members come the next meeting of our humble collect .

In anticipation of your reply. With many thanks Sir , Or Lady , my dear .

Major D F Clampywick (retired) .

Secretariat
30 Vincent Square, London SW1P 2PE

T 020 7821 3034
F 020 7821 3020

andrewsmith@rhs.org.uk
www.rhs.org.uk

Royal
Horticultural
Society

5 August 2009

Major D F Clampywick (ret)
President
The Devon Parsnip Alliance
Copperwalls Lodge

Devon

Dear Major Clampywick

Parsnips

Thank you very much indeed for your letter of 27 July 2009. On behalf of the
Society I am delighted to hear of your passion for parsnips and wish your group well
for the future.

Yours sincerely

Andrew Smith
The Secretary

The Manager .
JOHN LEWIS ,
The Mall at Cribbs Causeway ,
BRISTOL .
BS34 5QU .

Col .Charles Craftcake .
Copperwalls Lodge ,
DEVON .
23 - 09 - 2009 .

Dear Sir ,
      I have had the great pleasure to visit your store on numerous occasions . Each time has been a most pleasurable experience , apart from that is , the visit I made last Saturday 19-09-2009.
I had been perusing furnishings and had cause to make an enquiry of a member of your staff . The young lady I spoke to was most helpful , and indeed , delightful in her manner .
The young man I saw , some distance away from her , was writing something on yellow 'post it ' notelets . I took this young man to be an assistant in your store .
I thought no more of the encounter until I arrived home late that afternoon . It was when I removed my jacket in my own hallway that I saw a yellow ' post it ' notelet affixed to the back of my jacket .
The notelet read - "I am a miserable old Bastard" .
You can imagine my annoyance .
May I suggest that you examine the CCTV footage in the furnishings department at around 1.35 to 2.45 in the afternoon of that date . The identification of the miscreant would be appreciated . I would dearly love to tear the boy off a strip , for his behaviour , and give him a jolly good piece of my mind .
I have no desire to see the lad out on his ear , but a swift , (metaphoric) , kick up the backside would not come amiss from your good self , being his commanding officer and all that .
Jolly japery and high jinks are nothing new to me , being as I am , an old soldier having served Queen and country for some years . I can recall many practical jokes played , both by and indeed to , ones junior officers both overseas and at barracks .
I cannot recall , however , being called a miserable old Bastard .
Between your goodself , and I , the sentiment may have a grain of truth in it . However , I reserve the right to be so , and never to be called so .
Leave it with you my man . I eagerly await your reply .

I am sir , and shall remain , an admirer of your good works .

Col Charles Craftcake . (ret)

ohn Lewis

7 October 2009
MJ/B/023

The Mall at Cribbs Causeway
Bristol BS34 5QU

Telephone 0117 959 1100
Fax 0117 958 1326
jl_cribbs@johnlewis.co.uk

ol C Craftcake
opperwalls Lodge

evon

ear Col Craftcake

ank you for your letter dated 23 September and firstly, may I begin by apologising for the
lay in responding to you.

was absolutely delighted to read that you are an avid fan of John Lewis and you have all
und the service to be of a very high standard and indeed on your visit to our store on
turday 19 September, by the young lady who you dealt with. It is therefore most upsetting
d concerning to read of the experience that followed. As I am sure you will understand we
ll take a very dim view of any such behaviour by a Partner as described in your letter.

reviewing our CCTV footage for that day, unfortunately there was nothing that happened
t seemed untoward and therefore you will appreciate that unless you can provide me with
ore detailed description of the Partner, it is very difficult for me to make an identification.

ce again, please accept my profuse apologies for what has occurred and I was pleased to
d that you will still remain a loyal John Lewis customer. I would also like to thank you for
ur opened minded view of the situation and please do not hesitate to contact me if you have
more details.

urs sincerely

n Johnston
nager
tomer Service

il   JL_cribbs@johnlewis.co.uk

Tim Johnston (Manager) .
JOHN LEWIS ,
The Mall at Cribbs Causeway ,
BRISTOL .
BS34 5QU .

Col .Charles Craftcake .
Copperwalls Lodge ,

DEVON .

09 - 10 - 2009 .

Dear Mr Johnson ,

It would seem that my letter of September 23rd is invalid , and indeed , unwarranted .

Sir , I apologise unreservedly , it would seem that my very own Grandson , Billy , who was visiting for the weekend is the guilty party . The boy , as boys are , is a bit of a wag and affixed the ' post it ' notelet to my back as I arrived home on the date mentioned .

Billy , a proper lad , has been severely admonished , and has undertaken to desist from such activities in the future .

I must take some of the blame myself , as I have often played the odd prank on the lad , screwing his latest fashion trainers to the garden gate . Pushing his face into his seventh birthday cake and the like .

These days , being a couple of years older , he is hitting back with some stylish and not inconsiderable vigour .

The Grandson in question , that very same weekend , also thought it hilarious to swap my heart pills for tic tacs .

The boy also put a bottle of one's vintage port in the freezer . Mrs Thompson , the charming lady at our local Bakery , refuses now to serve me , this , only a week after the boy was sent for the bread . Heaven alone only knows what he may have said . I did expound my admiration for the good lady's diligence , and customer service prowess , which are second to none . Happily the lad lives in Buckinghamshire , and his visits are rare , my preparations for his next visit have already begun . Let hostilities be rejoined around Christmas time .

I do hope sir , that you did not march through the Furnishings department with your arse kicking boots on , it was , in this instance unnecessary . Your staff sir , are among the finest in the realm , and I am sure that they shall remain so .

Mr Johnston , again , my profound apologies . I would appreciate your confirmation sir , that no one , in your good staff were troubled by my groundless complaint in the first instant . I crave your reply , I am sir , fighting well below , but in fact , (I fear) well above my own weight .

Yours sir , with abject apology , and at your service ad infinitum .
Col Charles Craft cake (ret).

ohn Lewis

Cribbs Causeway

The Mall at Cribbs Causeway
Bristol BS34 5QU

Telephone 0117 959 1100
Fax 0117 958 1326
jl_cribbs@johnlewis.co.uk

7 October 2009
MJ/023

ol C Craftcake
opperwalls Lodge

evon

ar Col Craftcake

ank you for your letter dated 9 October 2009. I was very pleased to read that you have got
the bottom of the little mystery surrounding your visit to us on the 19 September. Thank
u for being so open and honest with us and you can rest assured that nobody has been
rimanded at this end.

 look forward to being of service to you when you are next in the area. Thank you once
in.

urs sincerely

 Johnston
ager
tomer Service

Partnership

RITZ CRACKERS .
Craft foods UK ,
FREEPOST SWC 3320 ,
CHELTENHAM GL50 3ZZ .

Emeritus Professor Grayson Clay .
The Institute of Cracker Research ,
Copperwalls Lodge ,
DEVON
09 - 11 - 2009 .

Dear Fellow Cracker Scientist ,
We humble few at the Cracker Research
Institute have arrived at a momentous conclusion .
The Ritz Cracker is the ultimate Cracker for Cheese .
Your product was subjected to rigorous , and indeed , vigorous and
extensive testing procedures .
Many rival crackers cracked , and in fact smashed , under test pressures .
The Ritz cracker withstood some , but could not withstand , the ultimate
smash of a well presented set of molars , incisors and canines working in
conjunction to crack a good crispy cracker . You'r product consistently
outcracked all of the rival brands time after time . Well done !
Some other , inferior crackers , cracked early , some cracked late , the
latter crackers left minor , but not insignificant injuries to our cracker
testers . The Ritz crackers harmed no-one , and were declared delicious
by 97% of our test group . The test group comprised of 33 random
persons , hauled from the street , and regardless of their consent to
participate .
The only failure we encountered in this particular test sample , was a man
who professed to have no teeth at all , and therefore asked to be exempted
from our research .
We tested his teeth , and found he was unable to break a cracker , even
under the most vigorous pressures that were applied to his head .
His complaint was disqualified , as when struck about the head , the
Cracker did , in fact , break .
His name was Mr Terrance Evans (a local Plumber) , of some repute .
A successful cracker will yield to a pressure equal to that which is exerted
by the normal human jaw , furnished with the requisite set of teeth ,
however , it may stay whole if that jaw is exerted by a parrot .
Nevertheless , a Rabbit jaw will smash any cracker . As will an average
Chicken . So will the average Pheasant , oh ! , it will , I have seen it .
The Institute Of Cracker Research has decided to send you a Certificate of
Excellence .
If , and when , our research establishment receives funds , the award will
be on its way to you , and well deserved it will be too .

Yours Sir , or Madam , with great admiration .   Grayson Clay .

Ref. No. *10821568*

Ms Grayson Glay
The Institute of Cracker Research
Copperwalls Lodge

Devon

21 November 2009

Dear Ms Glay

Letters of praise are always good to receive, so thank you for taking the time to let us know how much you enjoyed Ritz crackers.

We do our best to maintain a consistently high quality for all our products and it's great to receive such appreciative comments about them.

Thanks again for writing.

Yours sincerely

Jenna Silva
Consumer Relations Team

FLEET STREET INVEST .
7th Floor ,
Sea Containers House ,
20 Upper Ground ,
LONDON .
SE1 9JD .

ELI HUGGINS .
Copperwalls Lodge ,

DEVON .

22 - 09 - 2009 .

Dear Sir ,
     Being a crusty old type , (worker on the land) , through all
weathers and a world war . A proud man who made his living from the
land . I have no need of banks and the like .
I be here for over 67 year now , and never had a bank account , I always
pay in notes .   My Granddaughter , Paige , tells me I'm an old fool .
I already knows this . She says that I should get all that old money out
of those suitcases and into the bank . "Bugger it" , I says , but she wont
look after me no more if I don't . It was her that got me this www.
Computer , and its marvellous . She be the future . I be leaving her a
few quid when I fall off the old muck heap . I got a load of old money
no longer in circulation . Old fivers and tenners and the like . I got a big
bag of pound notes from the time of Harold Wilson . Me and the old girl ,
she dead now , made plenty when we had the big pig business round
these here parts . She ran the job , I just fed the swine , sold a few , and
killed a bugger or two for the eating , and meat selling like . Well I got
quite a bit now , cash that is , what you think then ? .   You got some
flash lads that will make this wedge into a lot more .
Paige is a bit of a modern girl , she got near on a GCE , she don't stink
one bit , not like the rest of them up there . They all bad buggers , and all
want their hands on my money . They aint getting it .
Paige reckons if I don't invest in something I could be missing out .
She says I got about threequarters of a million in notes here . Maybe she
has a point .   Got any ideas ? . You flash boys from London with yer
fancy suits must be able to come up with something .   Your on 2% . No
more son . I be looking for cast iron investment boy .
Let me know lad . If I don't like it , be sure I will let you know .

Yours sincerely ,   Eli Huggins .

FLEET STREET PUBLICATIONS LTD

Sea Containers House, 7th Floor
20 Upper Ground, London SE1 9JD
Tel: 020 7633 3600 Fax: 020 7633 3740

Mr Eli Huggins
Copperwalls Lodge

Devon

Thursday, 22nd October 2009

Dear Mr Huggins,

Thank you for your recent letter.

It is good to hear you are interested in investing. We have various publications and subscriptions on offer which can advise you in all aspects of investing.

Unfortunately we are unable to provide financial advice on a personal basis. We can only comment on our recommendations contained within our subscriptions. If you would like further information on the publications we have on offer to help you with your investing future please see our website www.fleetstreetinvest.co.uk.

Should require any further information please do not hesitate to contact us either by telephone or letter.

Kind Regards

Claire Roberts
Customer Services Representative

JBA (Seed Potato Specialist) .
Rosefield Farm ,
Old Carlisle Road ,
ANNAN ,
Dumfries & Galloway
DG12 6QX .

Mr H W Cylinder .
Copperwalls Spudlodge ,
DEVON.
03 - 05 - 2010 .

Dear JBA ,

    I have had for my dinner tonight , a delightful brace of local pheasant , accompanied by fresh vegetables from one's garden , and Maris Piper potatoes .

Damned delicious .

The Maris Piper , is of course , a waxy / floury textured potato with a creamy coloured flesh . We , the aged Lioness and I , frequently have them roasted , mashed , and indeed as chips .

Tell me please , if the crop is known to produce heavy yields . I ask this , as I intend to instruct Fat boy Huggins , our handyman , to grow some Maris Piper in the garden this year .

We have traditionally grown King Edwards , and although we are quite pleased with them , it is time for one to have a change .

Out with the old buggers , and in with the new .

(If only we could do that with the old mares when they get clapped out) .

The King Edward , of course is a white , roughish sort , with often a knobbly odd shape and pimply skin , a bit like her ladyship in fact .

Could do with a bally change there as well .

Are the Maris Piper -

A . More prone to blight .

B. Do they store well .

C. Can one bake them .

And .

D . Do you have any analysis on gravy absorption etc .

Will the old girl have any trouble in the microwavable apparatus when producing jackets .

Do hope you can answer the above enquiries .

Many Thanks in anticipation of your good advice

Mr H W Cylinder .

JBA Seed Potatoes
info@jbaseedpotatoes.co.uk

T. 01461 202 567
F. 01461 205 974

Dear Mr Cylinder

Thank you for your enquiry.

I can confirm that Maris Piper will produce large yields of floury tubers and will make excellent chips,
roasties and mash.

They are slightly better for blight resistance than the King Edwards and they store very well.
I have not tried to bake them myself but I would assume that the larger tubers would be good to bake.

Give them a try and let me know how you get on with them.

Best Regards

Iain Barbour

REED HUMAN RESOURCES BRISTOL .
Prudential Building ,
5 - 18 Wine Street ,
BRISTOL .
BS1 2PH .

Mr Lucas Harrison .
Copperwalls Lodge ,

DEVON .
12- 07- 2011

Dear Sir or Madam ,

        I am writing to you in the hope of receiving good advice . You are the leaders in the field of recruitment in Britain . It therefore , goes without saying , that your Human Resources department will be the most effective in sourcing quality employment . My quest for a suitable position has , for the last six months , been fruitless . Most employment advisors stress the need for more and more qualifications , and indeed for up to date relevant "modern" modules . I have qualifications in , and certificates for , the following ....

1. ITERPERSONAL SKILLS .
2. COUNSELLING .
3. COMMUNITY CARE (including ENB 939 requirements)
4. COMPUTER LITERACY .
5. FIRST AID . (severe blood loss response)
6. ASSERTIVENESS . (be there)
7. NON-VERBAL COMMUNICATION (including makaton)
8. BEHAVIOUR MODIFICATION (not including challenging behaviour) .
9. BEHAVIOUR MODIFICATION (including challenging behaviour)
10 CHALLENGING BEHAVIOUR (not including behaviour modification)
11. QUALITY ASSURANCE .
12. EQUALITY AND DIVERSITY (sexual orientation and preferences)
13. ENGLISH AS A FOREIGN LANGUAGE .
14. BASIC IRDU .
15. SELF DEFENCE (to commando level)
16. ADVANCED MANDARIN .
17. CONCRETE TECHNOLOGY . (levels one and two)
18. RISK ASSESMENT .
19. ANGER MANAGEMENT .

My Curriculum vitae , is , I would humbly suggest quite good . Your input would be priceless . Please give a snippet or two of advice .

Yours most sincerely , in anticipation of your assistance .

Lucas Harrison

REED
HUMAN
RESOURCES

Mr Lucas Harrison
Copperwalls Lodge

Devon

Dear Mr Harrison

Thank you very much for choosing Reed Human Resources to register your details. As a specialist agency focussing purely on the placement of Human Resources Professionals in the Bristol area, I regret to inform you that from this branch, we are unlikely to be handling any vacancies that will match your experience and skills.

I would advise you to visit our leading website www.reed.co.uk where you will find a wide range of vacancies for you to view and apply to. On our website you will also find contact details of your nearest Branch who recruit on behalf of clients for roles that will match your experience. I would also recommend taking time to add your career history on to your CV so that you more clearly demonstrate your experience.

Reed is one of the largest recruitment agencies in the UK. All of our offices are networked which opens up many more opportunities both locally and nationally to our candidates and our clients. One of the major benefits of having a large number of offices means we are able to develop excellent local market recruitment knowledge in the small to medium sized organisations as well as the larger blue chip companies.

We strongly believe that finding a suitable vacancy for a candidate is a two way process. We need to work together to enable us to find the most suitable position, as quickly as possible. We will provide feedback on the progress we are making on your behalf along with feedback after each interview. It is important you let us know of any changes in your circumstances after registering with us. Also inform us of any additional companies you would like us to contact on your behalf and / or do not want to be put forward to. Should you need to contact us, the best time is before 9am or after 4.30pm, as this frees us up to contact clients on your behalf, when they are most likely to be available.

We strive to provide the highest standards of service in our business. Indeed, many of our candidates register with us time and time again and also through recommendation - a sure sign of good service. Please do recommend us to your friends and colleagues, if you know of anybody else that we may be able to help. In the meantime, if you have any queries, please do not hesitate to contact us.

Yours sincerely

Anna Preston
Senior HR interims Consultant.
Reed Human Resources
0117 906 0009

Mr Boyce .
AT THE RACES ,
JAMES HOUSE ,
18 - 21 Corsham Street ,
LONDON N1 6DR .

Dennis Thornton .
Copperwalls Lodge ,

DEVON
13 - 04 - 2010 .

Dear Mr Boyce ,

    I am Dennis Thornton . , and I am 9 . When I get home from school on some nights , my dad has you and your programme on , and he watches the horse racing . Dad works from home and , "takes in the occasional race" , "if its on" . He says that there is a fantastic jockey called Andrew Thornton . He has almost the same name as me , is he really very good ? . He did ride a winner the other day , I saw it . And , he rode a Gold Cup winner .

There are a few things I must ask you , because of your authority on the matter and dad says you are one of the highest authorities in racing , second only to Gordon Broon , and he is over 7 feet tall my dad says . The questions are -

A . Is AP McCoy the greatest jockey ever ? .

B . Is Andrew Thornton the second best jockey ever ? .

C. Is Gordon Broon really over 7 feet tall ? . And , why do you always send him to Scotland , Does he like it there ? .

My mum , Gale , thinks you are very nice , my dad thinks you are ok , and I like your method of television broadcasting because you are sometimes quite funny .

Mum , Gale , would like a signed photo of you , but don't do it if you don't have the time . Dad says it has to be one with your best jacket on . Please do send me a reply , I am very much looking forward to getting a letter from a person on the television . I like you and will keep your letter forever . Good luck Mr Boyce , (Boycie) .

Thank you very much . And Yours Sincerely .

Dennis

Dennis Thornton .

Sean Boyce
ATR
18-21 Corsham Street
LONDON
N1 6DR

Dennis Thornton
Copperwalls Lodge

DEVON

Dear Dennis,

Thanks so much for taking the time to write in to ATR.

I think your dad might enjoy pulling your leg a little bit from time to time by the sound of it but your mum is clearly an excellent judge of TV presenters.

In answer to your questions, lots of people would agree that AP McCoy is the greatest jockey ever and certainly he's broken all the records for a jump jockey. I think he is an amazing sportsman and a great example of what can be achieved through really hard work and effort. He is also extremely determined and very brave. Away from the cameras he's also quite a funny fella too.

Andrew Thornton is probably not the second best jockey ever but as well as having an excellent name, he is an extremely nice guy. He is a jockey who really suits certain types of horses. I like to see Andrew riding horses that need to be ridden patiently and gently during races to get their jumping in a rhythm and finish their races powerfully. If you watch Andrew riding you'll notice that his stirrup leathers are longer than most jockeys which means he is perhaps more safety conscious than some of the younger jockeys and he doesn't like falling off. On the right type of horse he's very good indeed.

Gordon Brown is a very tall man but is a bit shorter than seven feet. I don't know his exact height but I would guess he's probably about 6' 2" or thereabouts. Gordon lives in the far north of England and he seems to like it there and of course being Scottish himself, he also enjoys covering the Scottish tracks. Another interesting fact about Gordon is that his hair seems to stay very tidy, even when it's very windy on the course. It's a good job he's never been to Devon because he'd discover how much nicer Devon is than the North of England and he mightn't want to go back. Devon is my favourite county and I often go on holiday there with my family.

Tell your mum that I'm very sorry but I don't have any photos of myself to sign but I'm very glad that she thinks I'm nice and that it's much appreciated.

Thanks again Dennis for taking the time to write in and I hope I've answered your questions for you.

All the very best,

- 111 -

Perfect Pets ,
56 Berners Street ,
IPSWICH ,
SUFFOLK .
IP1 3LU .

H Rommel .
Copperwalls Lodge ,

DEVON .

05 - 08 - 2009 .

Dear Dog Scientist ,
   Does your very excellent company provide a potion
to assist the poor hunder to , how you say , produce a firmen crappen .
The poor boy has much problem in that departments . Is loose you see ,
damp , high moisture level . All the time Monty is loose , The lawn is
brown , and my wife , Flaerters , wont let him back in the house until I
wash his legs .
Monty is off gravy and soup now , he eats good solid bone . Bone of
cow or pig . Arnold provides three or four bone a week for the lad. Oh ,
Arnold is our butcher , and good friend .
Monty is a clever dog and will kill anything he is commanded to , he will
destroy all rats and bunny with a glee .
Monty also won a obedient class with sweeping , aggressive , and
impressive lefts and rights , all to the command of the firm gripped hand .
I never beat Montgomery .
I am near a wits end . Monty is a good lad , but Flaerters is talking of
sending him to the police or the army , (he is a fine big Deutchland
sheppen) .
He is not a bit nasty , (unlike Flaerters) , and kids pat his back , My
daughter Gretchen loves him , but complaints about the smell sometime .
In conclude , the hunder needs repair , Flaerters has said him or me on
more than one occasion . " personally it's a toss of a deutchmark which
one I would choose" .

Please advise

Hans Rommel

why pay the vet price
you can pay the net price

petprescription

56 Berners Street,
Ipswich, Suffolk IP1 3LU
Tel: 01473 222392
Fax: 01473 231829
Email: info@petprescription.co.uk
www.petprescription.co.uk

Pefect Petcare Ltd
56 Berner Street
Ipswich
Suffolk
IP1 3LU

06/08/09

Dear Hans

Thank you for your recent letter, unfortunately I am unable to help on this occasion
with your dogs diarrhoea problems. I would advise that you contact your local
veterinary surgeon as there could be an underlying condition causing the problem and
this will obviously need to be ruled out.

Kind Regards

Jane Bartlettt BSc (hons) R.V.N.

Lost property office ,
BINNS DEPARTMENT STORE ,
7 HIGH ROW ,
DARLINGTON ,
Co DURHAM DL3 7QE .

Mr P Longdocker .
Copperwalls Lodge ,

DEVON
06-01-2009 .

Dear Sir / madam ,

      Whilst on a trip to Darlington , (Saturday the 20th of December) , to visit family and friends , I decided to have a look around your excellent store . It was during my time in Binns that I lost the button from my jacket . The button is red , measures some 35mm in diameter , and has 4 holes within it . The loss of this button is of great distress to me . I would like to recover it . Perhaps your CCTV coverage for that day could be examined , to ascertain exactly where the loss of the button occurred . I am a middle aged man , quite tall will lustrous grey hair . I am wearing a purple jacket ,with two buttons on it when I entered, yet only one button later . The time difference between my having two buttons , to the time I have but one , is crucial to this investigation . The time of my visit was approximately 3 p.m. to around 3.17 p.m. Whether you can find this button or not , please let me know as soon as possible . If I have indeed lost it for good , I shall have to try and start to rebuild my life without it . I do have another jacket .

Yours sincerely   Percival Longdocker .

P.S. I can send a photograph of the remaining button if it would help with positive identification purposes .

HOUSE OF FRASER

Mr P Longdocker
Copperwalls Lodge

Devon

9th January 2009

Dear Mr Longdocker,

With reference to your recent letter which was sent to our in store lost property department regarding your lost button.

Thank you for bring this matter to my attention, and I trust that you enjoyed your shopping experience whilst in the store. I have checked with our in store cleaning operatives and staff members regarding the lost button, and unfortunately we have failed to locate your lost property. I will however remind the staff that they should return the button to lost property should it be located after sending you this correspondence.

If I can be of any further assistance please do not hesitate to contact me.

Assuring you of our best intention at all times.

Yours sincerely

David Parkinson
Store Manager

BINNS 7 HIGH ROW DARLINGTON DL3 7QE TELEPHONE 08448003721 FACSIMILE 01325 382783 www.houseoffraser.co.uk

HOUSE OF FRASER (STORES) LIMITED REGISTERED OFFICE GRANITE HOUSE 31 STOCKWELL STREET GLASGOW G1 4RZ REGISTERED IN SCOTLAND NO 10677

The Public Relations Officer .
Stern & Co Accountants ,
12 - 15 Hanger Green ,
Ealing ,
LONDON W5 3AY .

Sidney Twent .
Copperwalls Lodge ,
DEVON .
14 - 06 - 2010 .

Dear Sir ,
   I am 14 years old and soon to begin my examination career ,
beginning with GCSE , and hopefully A levels in time .
My Father , an actor , has told me that my ambition to become an
Accountant is a foolish idea .
He often sites the fact that a man in our Village , Mr Perkins , is an
Accountant , and he is a very dull man .   Mr Perkins is indeed very dull .

He does however , earn a good salary , and has a large house .
I have argued with my Father that , even if Mr Perkins was a plumber , or
an acrobat , a lion tamer , or a clown he would still be dull .
Father contends that calculating every move , counting every step , and
valuing every encounter has ensured Mr Perkins has remained single .

My Father earned £5000 last week , but had no earnings whatever for the
preceding month , saying he was resting . There is then , a good case for
having a steady , well paid job .
Father often mentions job satisfaction , and creativity in his work , but his
last job was for a toilet roll company . I failed to find the creativity .
Does Accountancy get creative at times ? .
I have heard of creative accountancy , but do not understand it .

Is Accountancy a sound career option for a young chap ?
Father says you will not reply to this letter as there is no fee in it .

Please prove him wrong , I am seriously considering this as a career , so
any advice you have for me would be appreciated .

Yours Sincerely , Sidney Twent .

Our Ref: SP

Stern & Company

Chartered Accountants, Tax Consultants & Business Advisors

15 June 2010

12-15 Hanger Green
London W5 3AY

Tel
+44 (0)20 8354 9000
Fax
+44 (0)20 8354 9010

E-mail
admin@stern.co.uk

Mr Sidney Twent
Copperwalls Lodge

Devon

Dear Sidney,

Thank you for your letter dated 14 June 2010.

I can certainly advise you that accountancy is a sound career option for any young person. The training can be long, hard and boring even but it is rewarding when you finally achieve qualified accountant status. A lot of the work especially in the early days of your career can be quite boring but as you gain more experience and proficiency the work would become more interesting and even creative! There are a large number of different areas within the field that you can specialise in depending on your interests once you qualify. There can be a large amount of job satisfaction within accountancy, for example at the end of a long and complicated audit successfully completed.

Our firm is certainly not dull and boring as you can see if you have a look at our website. If you are ever in London you are welcome to come and see us so we can prove it in person.

We wish you very success in the future no matter what career path you decide to pursue.

With kind regards

Yours sincerely,

Sangita Patel
Manager

www.stern.co.uk

Julie Green .
Film Education .
91 Berwick Street ,
LONDON . W1F 0BP

Christopher Critic .
Copperwalls Lodge ,
Whitestone ,
DEVON EX4 2HT .

Dear Ms Green ,

I am nearly 10 and want to be a film critic .
My name is exactly right to be a critic .
Our School , Longbottom Lane primary , is not going to enter the
competition that you are running "Schoolsfilmweek" .
I want to enter , that is why I have to write to you direct , our School is
rubbish . My dad calls it a " Fagins academy " .

We have some right old thickies in our School , but a few of us are more
clever , and more articulate than our peers . We intend to get careers in the
job most suited to our names .   Like ..
Daniel Swindell , is going to work in a bank .
Ben Piper , is going to be a Plumber , (his dad already is) .
David Baker , is going to be a Baker . (his dad isn't) .
Steven Macmillan , says he will be Prime Minister on day , (there was one
in the 1960s) , I fear for our Nation if he does .
Clarissa Game , will follow her Mother , and go on the game .
She was an Athlete .   (She represented England in the 1987
Commonwealth Games)
Gordon Large , Is going into Show biz , like his dad , who is Laurence
Large , and he is a dancer in ladies company .
I have seen Gordon's dad , and he Is not a very good dancer .
Dean Fletcher , says there is little use for arrows these days , we have told
him he will starve to death . Unless he learns Bricklaying .

So , Ms Green , can you send to me , the advice form , the application
form , the teacher signature form , and any advice from an underprivileged
school form .
My School has many advantages , says the Head , I have yet to see them .
Lets prove the locality wrong , and bring some long awaited success to this
little corner of the Realm   .

Yours , most sincerely , Ms Green .   Christopher Critic .

Chris

film education

Christopher Critic
Copperwalls Lodge

Devon

Dear Christopher,

Thank you very much for your letter regarding our Young Film Critic competition, which my colleague Julie Green forwarded to me.

All the information you need to enter the competition can be found at www.youngfilmcritic.org but in case you don't have access to the Internet I have printed out all the relevant information for you and have enclosed it with this letter. You can post your entry to us at the address below or send via the electronic entry form on the website above.

I hope you are able to encourage your class to take part despite their varied career choices.

We look forward to receiving your entry.

Yours sincerely,

Lucy

Lucy Witcomb
YFC Coordinator

Ms Huntingford .
Human Resources Dept ,
Dorset County Council ,
County Hall ,
DORCHESTER .
DT1 1XJ .

Mr Harold Harris .
(Hilarious Harry) ,
Copperwalls Lodge ,
DEVON .
EX4 2HT .
03 - 09 - 2010 .

Dear Ms Huntingford ,

Following my interview with you on Friday the 27th
of August 2010 , I write to confirm my acceptance of the position of
Entertainments Officer , with the salary of £37500 per annum .
May I say my decision was not difficult to make after hearing the exciting
plans that you have .
Staff , and Student morale will undoubtedly soar in the first weeks of the
morning shows . We might even get a couple of Accountants smiling .
The plans I outlined in my interview are now complete , and I shall begin
on my very first day Monday the 13th of September with Banjo hour from
just before 9 am , then into the " staff challenge " .
I will , as suggested , bring along some costumes and funny hats , badges
etc , and these will be invoiced separately as agreed .
Day one has a multitude of surprises as promised , with balloons and Hairy
Terry , along with Gordon Goon and his gang of goons .
Silly Billy was booked for the Monday , but is being re-stuffed on that date
and cannot make it immediately after such an invasive procedure .
I have his assurance that he is free for his goose routine on Tuesday .
Smelly Kelly's leg has been re-attached and will be in the act on Friday .
The rest of the first week is taken up by my Vent act , Kevin and Kevin ,
(they are so similar) . I do propose to introduce Charlie the Chimpanzee
Chancellor on Wednesday , but recalling some disquiet from the interview
panel , this may be unwise to portray the Chancellor as a Chimpanzee in
the current economic climate , please advise me on the Tuesday if we
should use Charlie or not in that show .
In the unlikely event of any gaps in the performances , (lack of personnel
or Student involvement in the first week) , then Kevin and Kevin , (they
are so similar) , will step in to fill the breach .
Let me tell you , I cannot wait to get started , Should I report to reception
on Monday morning , or are there other arrangements for my first day ? .

I look forward to your reply with my instructions .

Yours   sincerely ,   Harold Harris .

Human Resources
County Hall, Colliton Park
Dorchester
Dorset DT1 1XJ

Telephone: 01305 221000
Direct line: 01305 224090
Fax: 01305 224411
Minicom: 01305 267933
Email: s.huntingford@dorsetcc.gov.uk
DX: DX 8716 Dorchester
Website: www.dorsetforyou.com

Date: 14 July 2010
Your ref:
My ref: SH/mmw

Mr H Harris
Copperwalls Lodge

DEVON

Dear Mr Harris

Further to your letter dated 8 July 2010, I write to advise that Rowland Hartle retired from Dorset County Council some months ago and we cannot find a recruitment record relating to yourself.

Yours sincerely

Sheralyn Huntingford
Head of Human Resources

Director for Corporate Resources Elaine Taylor

INVESTOR IN PEOPLE

- 121 -

Conservative Headquarters .
30 Millbank ,
LONDON SW1P 4DP .

Kirsty Bale-Carruthers ,
Copperwalls Lodge ,

DEVON
27 - 07 - 2009 .

Dear Sir or Madam ,
        Allow me to introduce myself , my name is Kirsty ,
and I am 9 and a half . Mummy is quite keen on politics and talks about
it all the time . She says that there are 3 main parties in England , they
are the Conservative party , the Labour party , and the other one that
does not matter . Mummy says that soon Mr Brown will not be the Prime
Minister anymore and that it will be Mr Cameron . BUT , if there is 3
parties then it could be the other one , or is this just silly talk as my
Mother says .
At the top there is The Queen , then it is Mr Brown , then it is Mr
Cameron , then who ?. Daddy says that it is Lloyd George or Jeremy
Thorpe . But I think Daddy wants to sell them to some other country ,
because he often says that they should be flogged . And sometimes
flogging is too good for them . He also says , (all the time) , that Mrs
Thatcher was the best Prime Minister we ever had .
If Mr Cameron wins the election , will he then be second in importance ,
only to the Queen herself . Daddy says that Mr Brown will have to go
and sell meat pies for a living then , but I don't think that is true .
I like Mr Cameron . Can I have a photograph with his signature on it
please . Mummy will be pleased .
I wish you good luck in your election complaining . I do hope you win
otherwise we are moving to Bolivia Daddy said .

Lots of love , Kirsty .

Kirsty

Rt Hon David Cameron MP
Leader of the Conservative Party

Kirsty Bale-Carruthers
Copperwalls Lodge

DEVON

Thursday, 13th August 2009

Dear Kirsty,

Thank you for your letter of 27th July to David Cameron telling us what your mummy and daddy think about politics and asking for a signed photograph.

Mr Cameron is a very busy man and he gets lots of letters and e-mails each week asking for photographs he has signed. I am sorry but because we have sent out so many signed photographs we no longer have any left and I don't know when we are going to get any more.

Thank you once again for your letter and I am sorry that you are going to be disappointed but I hope you will understand.

Yours sincerely

Jenny Stoker

Jenny Stoker
Office of the Leader of the Opposition.

David Cameron's Office, House of Commons, London SW1A 0AA Tel +44 (0)20 7219 6386 Fax +44 (0)20 7219 0360 www.conservatives.com

Public Relations / Educational Resource Dept . Ivan Westerly .
The Yorkshire Evening Post ,   Copperwalls Lodge ,
PO BOX 168 .
Wellington Street ,   DEVON
LEEDS LS1 1RF .   08 - 07 - 2010 .

Dear Sir / Madam ,

      My name is Ivan , I am 10 years old , and attend
Pargetter Junior School for boys in Mid Devon .
Over the coming holiday weeks we are to research a project on
" The Regions of England " . Most of the boys are to do Devon or
Cornwall , all a bit easy , some are to do Dorset or Somerset . Again a bit
easy to do , as some boys have relatives in the neighbouring counties , who
will act as resource for their studies . I am , however , a little different as
my family is more disparate . My Grandfather , now sadly deceased , was
in fact a Yorkshireman . A good and hardworking man .
I have decided to research my Grandfathers county for my project .
May I therefore , ask that you give some assistance if you can , and indeed
some advice if appropriate .
Grandfather used to say , EE BAH GUM LAD , and would call a hole in
the wall , or floor , AN OYL . He would also advise my Father to , TEK
THEE CAP OFF LAD , as an advice to remove his headwear .
His favourite saying was , THA CAN ALLUS TELL A
YORKSHIREMAN , BUT THA CAN'T TELL IM MUCH .
He would also refer to a Cricket Batsman who had been dismissed , and
would say , " GET THEE BACK T' PAVILLION LAD , AND TEK THEE
CAP OFF " .
My Father , an Accountant , would admonish him for expounding such
crudities , by saying " one is not in Yorkshire now dear Father " .
Daddy can be somewhat snoblike . I think he may be after an MBE .
Grandfather was , as many say , " the salt of the earth " , he was indeed a
magnificent man , large and strong with very hard teeth . He ate an almost
raw section of beef once , he really did , ...I saw it .
Granddad once said to me that he was considered for the part of The
Incredible Hulk , but was turned down , because he was just too big and
powerful . This was just a joke , but he was very strong , and looked very
fierce , and he NEVER , removed his flat cap .   Other than , presumably
for ablutions , and to go to bed .   He was a great man .
In conclusion sir , could you confirm , or indeed correct those sayings and
non correct English words , used as local dialect , or are they real ?.

Yours sincerely Sir , in the hope of good advice ,   Ivan Westerly .

YORKSHIRE POST
NEWSPAPERS LTD

PO Box 168, Wellington Street, Leeds LS1 1RF
Tel No: 0113 243 2701 Fax No: 0113 245 2410 : DX 25151, LEEDS 4

Mr Ivan Westerly
Copperwalls Lodge

Devon

Dear Mr Westerly ,

Please accept our apologise for the late response to your Letter.
Unfortunately our Educational Resources Department no longer exists .

Your correspondence has found its way into my in-tray in the last week. From the
information contained in your letter I understand you are at present researching the
county of your grandfathers birth as part of a school project .

To help you with your project please accept with our complements the
accompanying book, A Yorkshire Miscellany by Tom Holman . This is full of facts
about our great county . I trust you will find this of interest .

Yours sincerely

Paul Bolton
Reader Offers Organiser
Yorkshire Post Newspapers

Cathedral City cheese ,
Dairy crest ,
CLAYGATE HOUSE ,
LITTLEWORTH ROAD ,
ESHER ,
SURREY KT10 9PN .

Chardonnay Madonna Trotter .
Copperwalls Lodge ,
DEVON .
28 - 11 - 2008 .

Dear sir or madam or miss,

      At Sainsbury's last week we bought a lot of your cheese , my granddad is always looking for a bargain , and the cheese was buy one get one free . So we got 2 . Granddad said he likes it strong , but I don't , he ate some on the same night and it got stuck in his teeth , the all fell out ! , stuck together . They are false teeth . I am nearly ten ,(10) , and I didn't even know he had someone elses teeth , but I did think they were a bit too good for a really old man , he is well over 50 . He said get that &*%$£ stuff away from me , he did eat a bit more later that week , he quite likes it I think . We , (my sister Jordan Katie and me) ,took some out to the chickens that we have in the garden, they ran off with the pieces and ate them all , My granddad hit the roof , (he didn't actually hit it) , he said its too expensive for those Buggers .

2 days later he said that the eggs we had for breakfast tasted a bit cheesy , I didn't think they did, but he says he knows best . I also gave a bit of the cheese to Boris , and he pulled very funny faces and ran all over the garden very fast , OH Boris our dog . He is a border collie , but granddad thinks he is a twant . Granddad is old and is always in a bad mood , except when he has had the port . He says if he doesn't get the port every night he will die , due to a very rare disease . I took some to school as well ,(cheese) , and the other kids thought it was good . I like it now , and will try to persuade granddad to buy more . He has loads of money because he won a pool a long time ago , and its worth a load of cash , he still has most of it my mum says because he is a tight fisted old toad . What is cheese made of ? . Does the cheese make you sleep funny if you eat it at night , Granddad says it does , or is that all the port ?

Yours faithfully Chardonnay Madonna Trotter

Miss Chardonnay Madonna Trotter
opperwalls Lodge

evon

eference Number
81203-000035

3/12/2008

ear Miss Trotter

an you for your lovely letter, in response to your question "Does cheese make you sleep funny"?

s an old wives tale that eating cheese at night can cause nightmares. A study in 2005 carried out by the itish Cheese Board revealed that eating cheese before bed will not only aid a good night's sleep but fferent cheeses will in fact cause different types of dreams.

0 volunteers took part in the week-long study, 72% slept well every night, 67% remembered their eams and none recorded experiencing nightmares after eating a 20g piece of cheese half an hour fore going to sleep.

eese contains an amino acid called tryptophan that has been shown to reduce stress and induce sleep cheese may actually help you have a good night's sleep.

me believe that the myth that cheese gives you nightmares may have originated from Dickens' enezer Scrooge, who blamed "a crumb of cheese" on his night-time visitations.

full details of the British Cheese Board study go to:

p://www.britishcheese.com/news.cfm?page_id=240

pe this answers your question.

nk you once again for taking the time to contact us. I hope you continue to enjoy Cathedral City ure Cheddar Cheese and I'm sending you a product voucher with our compliments.

rs sincerely

han Gaster
edral City Consumer Careline Advisor
line Freephone: UK - 0800 783 7281

Freepost , Cathedral City, Dairy Crest, SY1108, Telford, TF6 6ZA
Registered Office: Claygate House, Littleworth Road, Esher, Surrey KT10 9PN Registered in England and Wales, No. 3162897

The Schools advice Dept .
The British Pig Association ,
Trumpington Mews ,
40b High Street ,
Trumpington ,
CAMBRIDGE .
CB2 9LS .

Miss Victoria Short .
Copperwalls Lodge ,
DEVON .
20 - 07 - 2010 .

Dear Mr , or Ms Schools Advisor ,

We have broken up from School , but not yet , its on Friday .

But when we go back , in September , I think its the 13th , we have to do a Project . I mean have a project ready .

It is about Breeding , maybe a dog , maybe a cow , maybe a cat , maybe a rabbit , maybe a mouse , or maybe any animal .

We all know we eat Cows , and Pigs . And Sheep , AND Chickens , and other animals . BUT , All of the food chain is very complex .

When we go back to School , after Summer , (oh ! I am 10 next week) , we have to put in a Project about Breeding .

My Mother has said that all Breeding is completely natural .

My Dad says that Breeding can sometimes be a mistake .

I live in a Farming area , and the farmer here has told me that the Cows cannot choose their own Husband , in fact , A big Bull Cow is the Father of all of the little cows .

I think that is alright , Dad says it is commercial , and I understand it .

Chickens , and we keep Chickens , and all 17 of them like our Cockrell Michael .

But Pigs , I don't know anything about really , and Miss Robson has made it abundantly clear , (she wrote down abundantly) , that I must not use Chickens or Cows for my project , as she thinks I may have an advantage .

So I thought I should write a letter to the most important people in the Pig Breeding world .

Could I say that if you are a boy who is writing this letter back to me , that you ask a Girl to do it , so it is not too brutal , because Boys can be very rude some times .

Yours Very sincerely   Victoria Short .

- 128 -

President The Most Hon. The Marquess of Salisbury P.C. . D
Chairman: Robert Overend M.B.E.

Miss Victoria Short
Copperwalls Lodge

Devon

Dear Victoria

I enclose some leaflets. Please have a look at our website where you
will find lots more information about pig breeding.

Yours sincerely

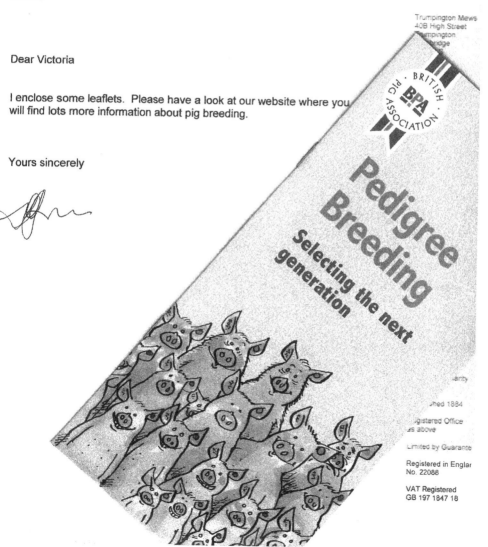

Trumpington Mews
40B High Street
Trumpington
Cambridge

Pedigree
Breeding

Selecting the next
generation

…anby

…shed 1884

…gistered Office
as above

Limited by Guarantee

Registered in England
No. 22088

VAT Registered
GB 197 1847 18

- 129 -

The Head Scientist .
Wall`s .
Unit 4 , Hampstead West ,
224 Iverson Road ,
LONDON .
NW6 2HL .

Emeritus Professor Giles Pommeroy.
The Sausage research Station ,
Copperwalls Lodge ,

DEVON
02 - 09 - 2010 .

Dear Fellow Scientist ,

We , at the Sausage research Station , have examined most exhaustively your product for quality and efficacy . We find that Wall`s Sausages pass with flying colours , our most stringent testing regime .

Naturally we test for safety , ease of use , texture , colour and value for money . The packaging , and instruction given thereon , both scored a maximum ten points . This is the first time this has happened . Congratulations !

The Sausage Research Station prides itself on the most rigorous of testing procedures found anywhere in the Sausage testing industry .

To pass this establishments tests is praise indeed , other sausages have failed the tests carried out at this station , some crumbled under the pressure , some cracked , many literally went Bang !

This Establishment uses , up to the moment laser technology , and the very latest in sausage penetration methods known only to the higher end of scientific testing .

I need not tell a fellow sausage aficionado that various sausage testing establishments may , at times employ shoddy and ineffective testing procedures , but not here .

Your excellent product is , I believe , the leader in the field of sausages . Again well done , your product is first class , If , and when , our Station creates , designs , and can afford to issue Certificates of excellence , be assured you will be sent one .

One of our Esteemed Scientists , here at " Sausage HQ " , has created an amazing artwork in watercolour , of Sausages .

It is basically a Landscape , or , more a Sausagescape , skilfully painted in the hazy , beautiful shimmer of twilight .

He calls it " Sausages at Midnight " .

It will have a limited print run of just 200 . Should you like one , please let me know , and I will advise you of the price , and conditions of purchase .

Yours most sincerely , carry on the good work , and well done
Professor Giles Pommeroy .

Giles Pommeroy
Sausage Research Station
Copperwalls Lodge

Devon

Dear Prof Pommeroy,

Thank you for your recent correspondence which we have read with great interest. Unfortunately I believe this is a case of mistaken identity. Here at Wall London we are retailers of luxury women's clothing and do not produce sausages.

I believe the correct recipient of your letter would be:

Kerry Foods,
Thorpe Lea Manor,
Thorpe Lea Road,
Egham,
Surrey TW20 8HY

Best wishes,

Wall London

Wall Luxury Essentials Ltd
Unit 4, 224 Iverson Road
London NW6 2HL
T 020 7372 7373
F 020 7328 7200
wall-london.com

Registered in England and Wales No. 33785500
Vat Reg No. GB 706 9314 34

Customer Enquiry Section .
Burtons the tailors ,
Colegrave House ,
70 Berners Street ,
LONDON W1T 3NL .

Mr T Thatcher .
Copperwalls Lodge ,

DEVON
17 - 08 - 2010 .

Dear Customer Enquiry Officer ,

My shopping experience with Burtons goes back many decades , and without exception, there has been full value for money given , with customer service second to none .

But , I have one small disappointment to report , and, although small , may still strike at the very heart of your very excellent company .

In preparation for the happy event of my wedding in 1974 , I wisely selected a shirt from Burton , a feint blue striped shirt , upon white . Resplendent in Pinstripe suit , (fashionable at the time) , I looked magnificent , If I do say so myself . Oh what a happy day .

I also bought an equally magnificent tie . It was , and still is , superb . Margaret , my new wife on that sunny day , divorced me 8 years later . No fault of the shirt obviously . (Nor the tie) .

Great happiness visited me again in 1985 , and having no finer garment , decided to marry wearing the shirt once more .

The tie was again a great comment gatherer .

Ruth , a fine wench , left not long after our second anniversary .

My current , and very lovely intended , Lillian and I will be tying the knot in late August , and do you know , when trying on the shirt , the damned thing had shrunk . This is very odd , as the shirt has been in the wardrobe , hung up and unused for nearly 25 years .

This shirt cannot now continue to play its part in the Thatcher tradition . I am shocked .

Soon to enter my 61st year , and my third marriage , I now have to buy yet another shirt , good heavens , how many shirts does a man have to get ? . I already have a plethora of casual shirts , but one , yes only one , getting married shirt . This was my lucky wedding shirt .

Has the shirt shrunk ? , the tie fit's as well as it ever did , (I purchased that in 1974 as well) , and I may have to accept that I may have put a pound or two on , since those Marc Bolan , Mud , and Rubettes days of my first shirt purchase . (The flares worn that day have also shrunk) . Can you therefore assure me that , if I purchase a shirt for this wedding , that it will see me through one , or perhaps two or more legal ceremonies should it be necessary .

Yours sincerely , T Thatcher .

Arcadia Group Limited

www.arcadiagroup.co.uk

Customer Services   Fax   0845 121 4521
Freepost 21 LON 8551
London W1E 3BN

email: customer.service@arcadiagroup.co.uk

6 September, 2010
Ref: stedmag/547021

Mr T Thatcher
Copperwalls Lodge

Devon

Dear Mr Thatcher

Thank you for your letter dated 17 August 2010.

I was pleased to read you have made such good use our garments as stated in your letter.

We intent to provide quality goods at all times, and it is reassuring to hear that the shirt you purchased a number of decades ago is still wearable.

Our product range is continually updated, and while we no longer stock the item you purchased in 1974, your local store will be happy to assist you in choosing an appropriate shirt for your wedding.

Thank you for taking the time to contact us and I hope you will continue to enjoy shopping with Burton.

Yours sincerely

Gemma Stedman
Customer Service Advisor

Group Limited Registered in England Company No. 237511 Registered Office: Colegrave House 70 Berners Street London W1T 3NL

Mel Stride .
Member of Parliament .
(Central Devon) ,
House of Commons ,
LONDON .
SWIA 0AA .

Richard Emery - Root .
Copperwalls Lodge ,
DEVON .
02 - 09 - 2010 .

Dear Mel ,

Well done boy , your in , I voted for you as the man who ,
with your well educated colleagues , will get us on our feet again .
Big job son , we are in the bowels of the biggest recession in living
memory , and you have plenty of work to do .

It's pretty clear to me that you will have to get tough with the shirkers and
good for nothings , that blight this once mighty , and productive Nation .
If cages have to be rattled , and arses kicked , then do it . You have my
full support .
New boys , such as yourself , will no doubt get a bit of ribbing , head
pushed down the toilet , that sort of thing , from the bigger lads .
If a left hook is in order , then deliver it , we wont think less of you .

But , when that is all over , you will have to produce results .
My advice to you is to get tough .
Make your name now , and make it big , make it tough , and make it
uncompromising .
Get a cause and tear it right up my lad .
The Headlines might read something like , " Mel Strides through
Corruption " . Or " Mel Strides ahead with reforms " .
Don't start with a biggy like Education or Nuclear Weapons , start small
with the parking charges in Crediton , or egg prices in the rural areas .
I would however , advise you to get started fairly quick with a few
complaints about injustice , to get us ordinary Joe's on your side .
Then , you can firmly strap on your arse kicking boots , and march through
the bigger issues with heroic consequence .
I would appreciate a reply to this letter , outlining your ambitions during
this Parliament , to keep up with your personal progress .
You never know son , History might read thus , Blair , Brown , Cameron
then Stride .

Yours sincerely , Richard Emery - Root .

Mel Stride MP

HOUSE OF COMMONS
LONDON SW1A 0AA

Mr Richard Emery-Root
Copperwalls Lodge

Devon

Ref: MS/CW/2734
Please quote reference when replying.
Date: 21 September 2010

Dear Mr Emery-Root,

Thank you for your recent letter. I very much enjoyed receiving correspondence written with such good humour. You are right that a good balance must be achieved between continuing to campaign locally on issues that affect the day-to-day lives of local residents, particularly the protection of vital local services, and seeking change in national issues like education (where I have campaigned vigorously for a fairer deal for Devon's schools).

More than 1,500 residents have contacted me since May 6th, some with simple questions that can be answered quickly, and some with more complicated cases. My immediate aim is to respond to and progress these important as quickly as possible.

I very much appreciate you taking the time to write to me and I hope you will enjoy reading my Parliamentary updates, which will be distributed regularly in Central Devon to keep residents up to date with what I am doing, both nationally and locally.

Yours sincerely,

Mel Stride MP

Tel: 01392 823306 or **Email:** mel.stride.mp@parliament.uk